International Series in Advanced Management Studies

More information about this series at http://www.springer.com/series/15195

Nicola Cobelli

Innovation in Community-Based Private Practices Through eHealth

A Business Management Perspective

SIMA
Società Italiana di MANAGEMENT

Springer

Nicola Cobelli
Department of Business Administration
The University of Verona
Verona, Italy

ISSN 2366-8814 ISSN 2366-8822 (electronic)
International Series in Advanced Management Studies
ISBN 978-3-030-48176-6 ISBN 978-3-030-48177-3 (eBook)
https://doi.org/10.1007/978-3-030-48177-3

This Springer imprint is published by the registered company Springer Nature Switzerland AG
The registered company address is: Gewerbestrasse 11, 6330 Cham, Switzerland

To Francesca,
Giulia and Agnese

Foreword

Dr. Cobelli's *Innovation in Community-Based Private Practices through eHealth: A Business Management Perspective* could not be more timely. The recent global COVID-19 pandemic crisis reinforced the limitations of not only the Italian healthcare system, but also those of healthcare systems in other developed nations such as the United States, Germany, or France. Dr. Cobelli's book does a magnificent job highlighting particular areas of the Italian healthcare system that are in dire need of reorganisation and reconstruction.

What makes this book truly special is that Dr. Cobelli's insights stem from his multi-year practical experience as a former senior executive in the Italian healthcare industry. This is not an outsider trying to understand the industry by relying on others' perspectives, but truly one of the industry's top experts! As such, the reader will find very specific and timely healthcare system-related issues that Dr. Cobelli has identified, as well as practical approaches and solutions that can be implemented to successfully address these challenges. This book is a must read for anyone with a stake in the healthcare industry, including patients, industry managers, academics, and policy makers.

University of Mississippi
MS, USA

David M. Gligor

Preface

Over the last few years, the conviction that the healthcare system, especially in the most developed countries, needs reconstruction and reorganisation has been strengthening among the general population. Healthcare is a widely discussed topic among health professionals, academics, and politicians, and new information technology offers innovative tools that can help to solve the toughest healthcare challenges.

Therefore, it is of interest to discuss the crisis in traditional healthcare systems, which are under enormous pressure to provide sustainable and innovative ways of delivering healthcare services and products. As a matter of fact, traditional public health systems now count on the long list of services and products offered by private community-based practices (e.g. pharmacies, hearing centres, opticians, and private medical centres).

The changes in current healthcare systems are supported by an incredible revolution in terms of accessibility and availability of health information on the internet. As a result, the changing role of the patient is strongly linked to the use of information technology.

Under such a scenario, the topic of 'eHealth literacy' has emerged. There are many definitions of eHealth and no consensus around the underlying idea. It is a widespread concept, applied extensively in modern literature, and publications in this domain are growing rapidly. There have been many important contributions; however, most focus on informatic, public health, legal, social, and anthropological implications. This publication, instead, is aimed at community-based private practice actors, to provide them with research models that explain the reasons why eHealth tools are, or are not, adopted.

In this work—focused on services, applications, and expected benefits of eHealth—we intend, from a managerial perspective, to (a) investigate how eHealth is currently interpreted and applied in community-based private practices, (b) present a systematic review of the theoretical research models that have been developed over the last 10 years on eHealth, (c) identify the many innovative managerial implications of eHealth, and (d) explore the choices of adoption/non-adoption of eHealth applications, such as Telemedicine, through an original research study.

In line with these aims, Chap. 1 discusses the crisis facing traditional healthcare systems, which are under enormous pressure to provide sustainable and innovative ways of delivering healthcare services and products. This chapter focuses on the Italian healthcare system, and on the relevance to this country of new non-medical health professions, which supply new products and deliver new services. Most of these function as community-based private practices and serve as proper retailers. Thus, their work contributes to the operation of the National Health System, and they can take advantage of relevant new technological tools otherwise available only to the public National Health System.

Despite the real necessity for change, many studies have demonstrated that, in general, the adoption of eHealth systems is often problematic. For these reasons, in Chap. 2, research models developed to explore and evaluate choices regarding adoption/non-adoption of new technologies are presented. These aim at providing entrepreneurs and managers of community-based private practices certain insights and tools to understand the ways in which eHealth can be helpful and beneficial for all healthcare system stakeholders.

Chapter 3 focuses on Telemedicine, as a possible eHealth tool. More precisely, it describes the European context, and subsequently, focuses on the Italian context, where Telemedicine still appears to be difficult to understand and diffuse. The need for training and information on Telemedicine, followed by a rigorous cost–benefit analysis, is essential to comprehend the necessity of appropriate Telemedicine implementation.

Finally, the fourth and final chapter (Chap. 4) of this volume addresses the research that has emerged from the growing interest in Telemedicine in Europe and, more particularly, Italy. Despite the abundance of legislation to increase accessibility of Telemedicine, especially in pharmacies, there continues to be resistance from various Italian regions, rendering Telemedicine in Italy an isolated and sporadic phenomenon. As will be discussed in the preceding chapters, the diffusion of technological innovations in health systems is a crucial factor in the adoption of such innovations, which must be done consciously by community-based organisations. Hence, it is of interest to investigate the reasons why Italian pharmacists and owners or managers of community-based pharmacies choose not to adopt Telemedicine. As will be seen over the course of this chapter, respondents were neither uniform nor compact. Indeed, the survey, based on the unified theory of acceptance and use of technology, shows that there are profound differences among groups of respondents and a range of variables that come into play in the choice of whether or not to adopt Telemedicine. For example, the assumption that younger people would be more inclined to adopt technological innovations was not supported by the data, which indicate the exact opposite. Thus, this chapter will assist both public and private decision-makers to make appropriate decisions so that Telemedicine is no longer, in Italian communities at least, an episodic and sporadic phenomenon.

This work makes three main contributions in terms of originality: it examines eHealth from the perspective of healthcare community-based private providers, it provides a systematic review of the studies conducted on the topic, and it includes a chapter with an application of a recent research model applied to healthcare community-based private providers.

This book was originally conceived to address healthcare professionals (owners, managers, and employees) working in private community-based private practices since they are among the primary beneficiaries of the adoption of eHealth tools, such as Telemedicine. Certainly, the main objective of this work is to provide such professionals with managerial tools capable of improving the quality of their work. However, the social implications presented and discussed highlight the potential that innovation and digital innovation have to empower and make more effective health service providers (public and private health organisations), service users (patients), and their entire networks (families, peers, and even citizens).

Data collected and research conducted in times in which the National Health Systems are facing new challenges, such as the Covid-19 pandemic, are also of particular relevance. Certainly, today's conditions linked to the pandemic in progress suggest, if not even impose, that a correct innovation, made of a combination of healthcare professionalism, managerial tools, and ICT, represents a new way of making goods and services related to health still and even more available. In this scenario, data analysis presented in this book can become the starting point to examine how the provision of health products have changed during and will change after the Covid-19 challenge.

Verona, Italy Nicola Cobelli

Acknowledgments

This book would not have been possible without pharmacists—owners and managers of community-based private practices—who allowed me to develop and test insight-related ideas in projects, workshops, and consulting engagements over the last two years. Thank you, Dr. Mario De Biasi, for your suggestions and ideas, and mainly for your sincere friendship.

I owe an enormous debt of gratitude to those who gave me detailed and constructive comments on one or more chapters, including Prof. Vania Vigolo, Prof. Fabio Cassia, Prof. Angelo Bonfanti, Prof. David Gligor, and Prof. Lesley White. They gave freely of their time to discuss nuances of the text and pushed me to clarify concepts, explore particular facets of insight work, and explain the rationales for specific recommendations. I would like to thank Prof. Marta Ugolini, who, over the years, supported me in my work and stimulated me to pursue new and challenging areas of research. My gratitude goes to Prof. Federico Brunetti and Prof. Elena Giaretta for their warm-hearted exchange of thoughts and ideas.

I would like to thank Prof. Claudio Baccarani for his inspirational approach to management studies, and the colleagues at the Department of Business Administration, University of Verona, with whom I have the opportunity to work.

A heartfelt and sincere thanks goes to Prof. Gaetano Miceli and Prof. Maria Antonietta Raimondo. Your Summer Schools have provided the tools without which I would not have been able to analyse the data as presented in the course of the volume. Your suggestions and, above all, your modesty are and will continue to be a point of reference for me. Your school continuously helps young researchers and Professors to understand the black box of statistics, to understand which tools are really useful for research in the field of Social Sciences and, more precisely, of Business Management. Thanks to you, I managed to understand how Statistics and Business Management can go hand in hand, to give data collections a different and deeper meaning. The statistics you explain is not a simple list of Methods, but it drops into reality and helps both Academics and Managers to make research an interesting activity for research institutions as well as for private companies.

The contribution of anonymous reviewers was essential for the improvement of this book. I thank them, and thank you, Prof. Alberto Pastore, for believing in this project and accepting it into the *International Series in Advanced Management Studies*.

I wish to thank the Department of Business Administration of the University of Verona in Italy, for all the tools (libraries, electronic sources, and administrative assistance) made available during the hard journey of writing. My gratitude also extends to the Springer editorial staff.

I am also immensely grateful to Prof. Roberto Burro. He has constantly encouraged me to 'get that book done'. I cannot thank him enough for being an unrelenting source of inspiration to challenge how things 'get done'. Without your support, Roberto, this book simply would not exist.

Finally, I want to thank my wife, Francesca, and my daughters, Giulia and Agnese, for tolerating my incessant disappearances into my home office. You are the individuals I live for and I truly hope to deserve your love.

Contents

Chapter 1
Innovation Management, Healthcare Challenges and eHealth

Abstract Over the past years, the conviction that the healthcare systems, particularly in the most developed countries, need reconstruction and reorganisation has been strengthening. Therefore, it is interesting, in this first chapter, to discuss the crisis facing traditional healthcare systems, which are under enormous pressure to provide sustainable, innovative ways of delivering healthcare services and products. This chapter will focus on the Italian healthcare system and on the relevance in this country of new non-medical health professions, which supply new products and deliver new services. Most of these function as community-based private practices and are proper retailers. Thus, their work contributes to the operation of the National Health System, and they can take advantage of relevant new technological tools that are otherwise available only to the public National Health System. Moreover, the private nature of these practices offers them flexibility and agility, such that they are the first potential beneficiaries by their use of new technological tools. Indeed, an incredible revolution is occurring in terms of the accessibility and availability of health information, products and services through the Internet. As a result, the changing role of the patient is strictly linked to the use of information technology, in the context of the so-called eHealth field, a paradigm that will be discussed based on an extensive literature review, with the aim of defining the current position of the research, managerial and social actions and implications related to eHealth.

Keywords eHealth · Healthcare systems · Innovation management · Healthcare management

1.1 Innovation Management in Healthcare

A considerable body of literature (Adams et al. 2006) has investigated whether innovation is the basis of a competitive economy (Porter and Ketels 2003). This literature provides evidence that competitive success depends on an organisation's

N. Cobelli, *Innovation in Community-Based Private Practices Through eHealth*, International Series in Advanced Management Studies,
https://doi.org/10.1007/978-3-030-48177-3_1

management of the innovation process and proposes factors related to successful management of this process (Balachandra and Friar 1997; Cooper 1979; De Brentani 1991; Ernst 2002; Globe et al. 1973; Griffin 1997; Rothwell 1992).

Quantifying and evaluating innovation competence and practice is a significant and complex issue for many contemporary organisations (Frenkel et al. 2000). An important challenge is to measure the complex processes that influence the organisation's innovation capability to facilitate their optimal management (Cordero 1990).

According to Adams et al. (2006), in the innovation management literature, measures of the aspects of innovation management are frequently proposed, responding to the need of firms and academics to understand the effectiveness of innovation actions. However, organisations' actions are fragmented, and as found by empirical studies, a probable consequence of this fragmentation is that many organisations tend to focus only on the measurement of innovation inputs and outputs in terms of spend, speed to market and numbers of new products and ignore the intermediate processes (Cordero 1990).

Innovation management is particularly relevant and, thus far, has been underestimated when considering the healthcare industry. Health professions have the responsibility of the safety, effective care and appropriate treatment of patients and hence play a vital role in the delivery of healthcare. From a healthcare management perspective, healthcare organisations face major challenges, including suboptimal prescribing, poor patient adherence to prescribed medication regimens, adverse drug reactions and interactions, medication administration errors and inadequate communication across the primary/secondary care interface (White et al. 2011). Further, at a time of escalating healthcare costs, maintaining cost-effectiveness of healthcare treatments has become an imperative, especially because public expenditure accounts for the largest proportion of healthcare costs (Brown et al. 2016).

Many studies have demonstrated the importance, and even necessity, of the National Health Systems (NHSs) innovating to survive (Freed et al. 2018). Ensuring innovation in healthcare delivery is a critical requirement to address the related challenges of access, quality and affordability through new, creative approaches. Healthcare environments must foster innovation, not just by allowing it but by actively encouraging it to occur anywhere and at every level in healthcare, from the laboratory to the operating room, bedside and clinic (Lipworth and Axler 2016). Many studies review the essential elements and environmental factors required for health-related innovation to flourish in a health system (Lister et al. 2017; Miller and French 2016; Tamblyn et al. 2016). The literature asserts that innovation must be actively cultivated by teaching it, creating 'space' for it, supporting it and providing opportunities for implementing it (Dzau et al. 2013). Some authors seek to show the importance of these fundamental principles and the ways these can be implemented by highlighting examples from across the country and their own institution (Ellner et al. 2015; Lavoie-Tremblay et al. 2017; Snowdon et al. 2015).

Health innovation cannot be relegated to a second-class status by the urgency of day-to-day operations and patient care and by the requirements of traditional research. Innovation needs to be elevated to a committed endeavour and become a part of an organisation's culture, particularly in academic health centres, since innovation is defined as 'the intentional introduction and application within a job, work team or organization of ideas, processes, products or procedures which are new to that job, work team or organization and which are designed to benefit the job, the work team or the organization' (West and Farr 1990, p. 9). Thus, innovations are the result of a cyclical process, which consists of stages of idea generation and of idea testing and implementation.

Accordingly, as already stated, over the past years, the conviction that the healthcare systems, especially in the most developed countries, need processes of innovation—and more precisely, reconstruction and reorganisation—has been strengthening (Marmor 2013). Healthcare is a widely discussed topic among health professionals, academics and politicians. In fact, most healthcare stakeholders are persuaded that some action needs to be taken at any level, locally, regionally or globally (Kodama 2015). Thuemmler and Bai (2017) argue that delivering care as at present will be unaffordable for any society 20 years hence.

Therefore, it is imperative to discuss the crisis facing traditional healthcare systems. In fact, they are under enormous pressure to provide sustainable, innovative ways of delivering healthcare services and products (Perelman 2017). This crisis could be attributable to demographic evolution, cost escalation, technical development, an increasingly turbulent digital environment and, more broadly, the growing demand for health services and products.

A series of tendencies, mostly related to demographics and health expenditures, need to be investigated. Notably, many studies have highlighted that the changing configuration of patient groups due to developments related to demographic changes is among the main challenges for healthcare systems (Menvielle et al. 2017).

Life expectancy of the population in industrialised and in emerging countries has risen over the past decades, whereas—particularly in Europe and North America—fertility rates have been dropping. Life expectancy is projected to increase from 73.5 years in 2018 to 74.4 in 2022 (Morris 2019). These phenomena do not necessarily lead to a socio-economic problem, but in developed countries, where the birth rate has fallen sharply, the outcome is certainly an older population with fewer children.

Hillman et al. (2018) affirm that in Western countries, a 'silver tsunami' (i.e. the huge number of people who are moving towards retirement age) will drive the next 10 years of healthcare systems and that healthcare has to innovate faster than ever in these nations. Thus, as a result of the changing demographics, the demand for health services and products is increasing (Vitalari 2016), and the patterns of disease are transforming towards chronic illness because of the increase in the ageing population (Liao et al. 2017).

Undoubtedly, new health approaches that consider these demographic changes must be adopted. However, it is unlikely that the current healthcare systems and players will be able to bring about this transition without external support (Morris 2019).

Another relevant trend, linked to the way of delivering healthcare, is the one concerning healthcare costs. Healthcare development is considered a threat to the sustainability of the system and, simultaneously, a relevant economic development and a huge commercial opportunity for certain stakeholders, such as the pharmaceutical industry, insurers, ITC providers and new entrants, who are able to provide cost-effective, high-quality, safe and accessible healthcare services. This is another of the major challenges for health systems (Liao et al. 2017).

It is interesting to underline that the total expenditure on healthcare systems is growing faster than the gross domestic product (GDP) of certain countries and more rapidly in low and middle countries. In 2015, 10% of the global GDP was spent on health (Morris 2019). Public spending maintains its centrality in health coverage and shows a globally positive tendency, which started in the early 2000s. Meanwhile, out-of-pocket expenses have reduced (Morris 2019).

In addition, the data on per capita expenditures reveal important variations across all groups as well as strong inequality in terms of share of GDP among regions/country. The global healthcare expenditure is projected to increase at an annual rate of 5.4% in 2018–2022 (as against 2.9% recorded in 2013–2017; Morris 2019). Nevertheless, there are strong inequalities between countries and between geographical areas (World Health Organization [WHO] 2018). These disparities are also found in the misdistribution and shortage of healthcare personnel (Benkaouz and Erradi 2015).

Further, the method of financing healthcare systems varies across countries. Studies clearly show that high- and middle-income countries (e.g. European countries) tend to present a high share of prepaid sources (e.g. government budget from taxes and social health insurance). In low-income countries, public expenditure has declined from 33 to 20% of the total, following the increase in other resources (WHO 2018). As a result, the health sector is based on an unusual system of payments and reimbursements, which are normally made by a third party, which varies between countries. It is evident that the financial healthcare system and the related revenue streams are complex (Bukh and Nielsen 2010).

The trends described thus far confirm that it is necessary to adopt new and different approaches to health in accordance with regional characteristics and income level apart from other structural attributes. Moreover, socio-economic and demographic changes, as discussed, will support a deep structural change in the way healthcare is delivered in Europe, the United States, China and other countries (Thuemmler and Bai 2017).

In this study, we intend to investigate the approaches to be adopted to enable healthcare systems to overcome existing limitations. One possible solution is the digital transformation of these systems. Our focus will be on community-based private practices, whose relevance for end users is frequently underestimated. In many countries, the NHSs would cease to function without the existence of a parallel private activity. In this regard, Italy is an interesting case to study for three reasons. First, Italian governments have been creating and recognising new health professions since 1994 to supplement and regularise various non-medical health profiles. Second, in 2018, official orders were issued for these professions (Ministerial Decree n. 313th March 2018). Third, the Italian government, through the Ministry of Economic Development, has launched, with France and Germany, the National Industry 4.0 Plan, whose purpose is to develop, among other activities, the healthcare system in particular, with a focus on public health and on health community-based private practices based on new technological tools available currently. The National Plan provides fiscal advantages and funding possibilities for digital innovation projects in the healthcare sector as well (see Italy's national plan Impresa 4.0, n.d.).

1.2 Configuration of Healthcare System in Italy

Italy's NHS was created in 1978. Healthcare is provided to all citizens and residents by a mixed public–private system. The public part is the National Health Service, *Sistema Sanitario Nazionale* (SSN), which is organised under the Ministry of Health and is administered on a regional basis.

Prescription drugs can be acquired only if prescribed by a doctor. If prescribed by the GP, they are generally subsidised, requiring a co-payment that depends on the medicine type and on the patient income (in many regions, all the prescribed drugs are free, that is, for those whose incomes are below a certain threshold). Over-the-counter drugs must be paid for by the patient. Prescription and over-the-counter drugs can both only be sold in specialised shops, pharmacies or parapharmacies.[1]

Waiting times are usually up to a few months in the big public facilities and up to a few weeks in the small private facilities that have contracts to provide services through the SSN, although the referring doctor can shorten the waiting times of the more urgent cases by prioritising them. However, patients can opt for the 'free-market' option provided by these public and private hospitals, which they must pay for completely and generally has much shorter waiting times.

Although the SSN is configured to offer all citizens the same conditions, the limited expenditure capacity combined with the large number of new services and products available necessitated the creation of new health professions.

In 2017, the Italian National Statistics Institute (2017) disseminated for the first time the estimates on the system of health accounts for 2012–2016. The document, which is the most recent source of information, provides a framework for the country's health system that is useful for satisfying analytical needs. The system of health accounts was constructed according to the System of Health Accounts methodology and is in line with the accounting rules dictated by the European System of Accounts, ESA 2010. In 2016, Italy's health expenditure was €149,500 million, with an incidence on GDP of 8.9%; Fig. 1.1 shows that 75% of it was supported by the public sector and the remaining 25% by the private sector.

---

[1] Parapharmacies are springing up all over Italy, and there are about 6,564 in 2019. These were first promoted through Law Decree 4 July 2006 n. 223. A parapharmacy can sell over-the-counter medicines only and a huge variety of other products: personal hygiene products, cosmetics, diet foods, hair care products, baby products, beauty treatment products, homeopathic remedies, vitamins and products to help quit smoking. They also sell the non-pharmaceutical elements of a first-aid kit: plasters, tweezers, cotton wool and mild disinfectant sprays.

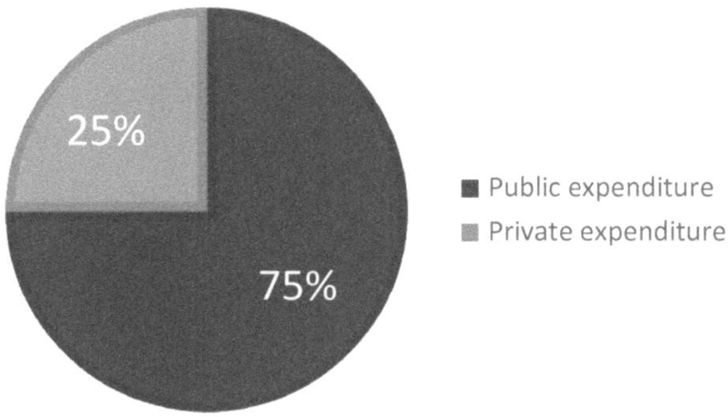

Fig. 1.1 Private and public expenditure in Italy (year 2016). Figure 1.1 shows that public expenditure on health is a major component of the total health expenditure in Italy, although a significant share of the total expenditure, that is, 25%, is the private expenditure incurred by households. Source: ISTAT, Il sistema dei conti della sanità per l'Italia, p. 1

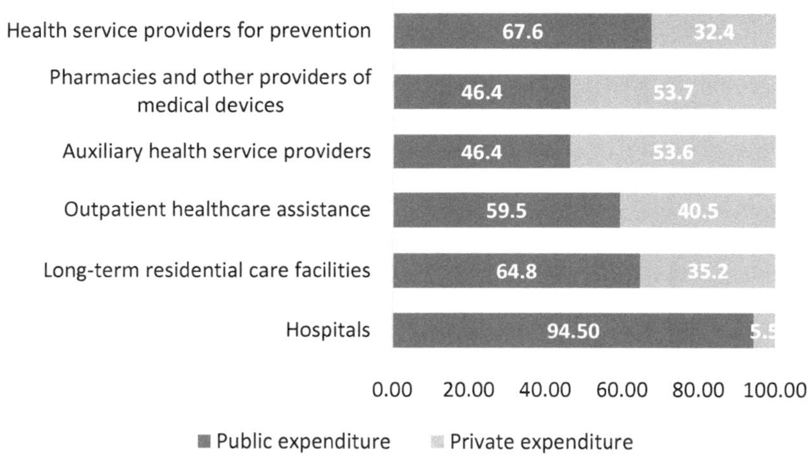

Fig. 1.2 Percentage balance of health expenditure by source of expenditure. Figure 1.2 shows the balance of private and public expenditure for items of expense. Hospitals are still the organisations where the NHS is investing more, but for all the other expense items, a certain balance can be observed when comparing public and private expenditures. Source: our elaboration on ISTAT, Il sistema dei conti della sanità per l'Italia, p. 5

Private healthcare expenses in 2016 amounted to €37,318 million, and its incidence as a proportion of the GDP is 2.2%. Families directly support private health expenditure. In 2016, health spending per capita was €2,466 and, compared with 2012, shows an average annual increase of 0.7%.

Figure 1.2 shows the proportion of both private and public healthcare expenditures. Hospitals are the main public expense, whereas the expenses on other items are balanced between private and public providers.

In Fig. 1.3, the household expenditure on separate items is detailed. Direct household spending on healthcare for rehabilitation and care increased by an annual

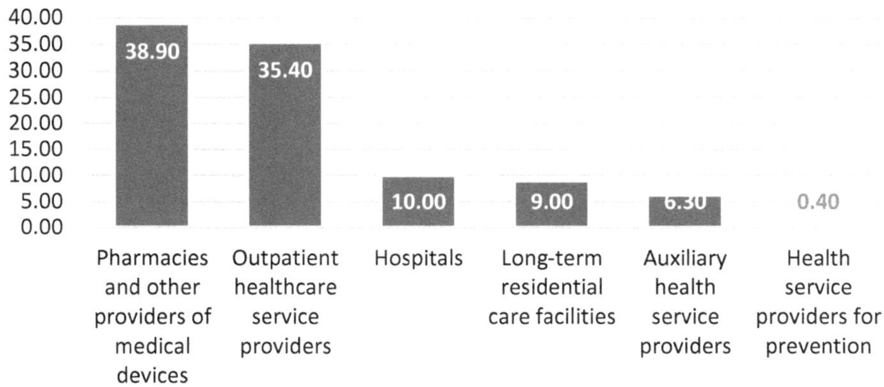

Fig. 1.3 Percentage of household health expenditure (year 2016). Figure 1.3 shows the relevance of the expenditure items 'Pharmacies and other providers of medical devices' and 'Outpatient healthcare service providers' for Italian families. Source: our elaboration on ISTAT, Il sistema dei conti della sanità per l'Italia, p. 4

average of 3.7% with a 4.4% growth in the outpatient component. The extension of the waiting lists in the public sector and the increase in the levels of the partnership (which increases the rates of the public sector to those of the private sector) seem to have influenced this change.

Overall, we can state that the SSN operates in combination with many community-based private practices, whose work ensures that patients can access the latest health treatments and thus supplements the services offered traditionally by the SSN itself.

In 2015, the Italian Senate produced a document titled 'Consultation on the sustainability of the healthcare system' ('Indagine conoscitiva sulla sostenibilità del Sistema Sanitario') in which the sustainability of the SSN was presented. In the report, the Senate outlined the main criticalities the SSN should address to achieve sustainability. The restrictions on healthcare expenditure, the deficit of some regions' balance sheets for which repayment plans were issued (De Belvis et al. 2012) and the periodic, heavy turnover of healthcare professionals (Shimizu et al. 2005) were depicted by the Italian Senate as possible causes of the high disparities in the provision of services by the regional healthcare systems. The 2008 economic crisis also affected health expenditure: health expenditure per person decreased by 3.5% in 2013 and 0.4% in 2014 (Brian 2015). Moreover, an increase in citizen co-payment on drugs (De Belvis et al. 2012) and in requests for private health services were the main consequences of a system not designed for quality and efficiency (Senato della Repubblica Italiana 2015). Examining these issues, some scholars indicated that information technology and private practices could help lift the healthcare system out of the crisis (Lavalle et al. 2015).

In Italy, academic centres are promoting courses of the so-called non-medical health professions since the 1990s. As per the government's plan, the graduate students of these academic degree courses are mainly employed by community-based private practices and not by the SSN. This is mainly because of the limited spending capacity of the SSN. Therefore, new or renovated forms of health business models have emerged (Cavicchi and Vagnoni 2017).

These models are used in relatively new professions, such as those created in 1994 with the Legislative Decree n. 319 and the subsequent Ministerial Decrees (D.M.), which identify the areas and professions presented in Table 1.1.

Moreover, such models are used in more traditional professions, such the ones of orthodontists and pharmacists.

Although all these health professionals are part of the NHS, since they are strictly regulated in terms of conditions and titles to operate, they work most of the time as independent contractors or own private practices.

From a business management point of view, it is relevant to highlight that in terms of the nature of their independency, these professionals tend to work in relatively new types of organisations, such as private medical centres, hearing care centres, health shops and rehabilitation centres. Some such practices have mutual agreements with the Italian NHS, but most function independently.

Very often, these new types of community-based private practices take the form of actual retailers. Digitalisation (Parviainen et al. 2017) is one of the most significant ongoing transformations for retailers, who provide consumers with various digital products and services that are adapted to the use of digital technologies and

Table 1.1 Non-medical health professions in Italy per area and sub-area with the detailed legislative framework

Area 1: Rehabilitative health professions	Legislative framework
Chiropodist	D.M.* 14.09.1994, n. 666
Physiotherapist	D.M. 14.09.1994, n. 741
Speech therapist	D.M. 14.09.1994, n. 742
Optometrist	D.M. 14.09.1994, n. 743
Neuro therapist and psychomotricity of the evolutionary age	D.M. 17.01.1997, n. 56
Psychiatric rehabilitation technician	D.M. 29.03.2001, n.182
Area 2: Technical health professions	Legislative framework
Audio therapist	D.M. 14.09.1994, n. 667
Laboratory technician	D.M. 14.09.1994, n. 745
Technician in radiology	D.M. 14.09.1994, n. 746
Technician in neuro-physiopathology	D.M. 15.03.1995, n. 183
Orthopaedic technician	D.M. 14.09.1994, n. 665
Audiologist	D.M. 14.09.1994, n. 668
Dental hygienist	D.M. 15.03.1999, n. 137
Dieticians	D.M. 14.09.1994, n. 744
Technician in prevention of workplaces	D.M. 17.01.1997, n. 58
Healthcare aide	D.M. 17.01.1997, n. 69

Source: our adaptation from http://www.salute.gov.it/. Accessed 16 Dec 2019
Table 1.1 shows a list of relatively new health professions introduced in Italy since 1994

are simultaneously affected by the new forms of consumption associated with these digital technologies. While digitalisation has a long history in retailing (Hagberg et al. 2016), the significance of the transformation is becoming increasingly visible in the healthcare systems as well, where the traditional doctor–patient relationship has dramatically changed for two main reasons: first, doctors are no more the only point of reference for patients, and, second, patients have become more empowered and demanding (Annarumma et al. 2017). If, in the past, the condition of health v. illness was very clearly defined, currently, citizens are more attentive to a grey scale, where health and illness are the opposite poles between which the condition of psychophysical well-being can vary greatly. In fact, the WHO (2013) defines health as a state of complete physical, mental and social well-being, and not merely the absence of disease or infirmity. Therefore, when viewed from the perspective of retail management, the healthcare system can be transformed by adopting new information technology tools. A neologism was created to define the vast number of new technological tools available currently for healthcare systems: eHealth (Gibbons 2007; Gibbons and Shaikh 2019). In the continuation of this research, we intend to propose some definitions of eHealth (Tan 2005) and then consider the issues linked to the adoption of these new technologies.

As shown in Fig. 1.4, according to Al-Fuqaha et al. (2015), healthcare organisations are those that can have a high economic impact from the application of new information and communication technology (ICT) web-based tools. In this sense, eHealth is potentially a very powerful solution that can enable healthcare systems to keep pace with the need of empowered, demanding patients.

Fig. 1.4 Potential economic impact of eHealth applications: projected market size in 2025. Figure 1.4 shows the projected market size of eHealth applications by 2025, where healthcare is the industry that might enjoy the greatest benefits from new information technology tools. Source: our adaptation from Al-Fuqaha A, Guizani M, Mohammadi M, et al (2015) Internet of things: a survey on enabling technologies, protocols, and applications. IEEE Comm Sur Tutor 17(4): 2349

1.3 eHealth as a Possible Innovative Approach to Healthcare Management

Many definitions of eHealth have been proposed, and consensus around the underlying idea is lacking (Gaddi et al. 2013; George et al. 2012; Hernandez 2009; Ho et al. 2012; Hörbst et al. 2014; Rosenmöller et al. 2014). This concept is applied extensively in modern literature (Showell and Nohr 2012; Blobel et al. 2012), and studies on this domain continue to increase rapidly (Fatehi and Wootton 2012). eHealth has its origin in the Internet and is related to the process of digitalisation that many industries are experiencing (Meier et al., 2013). The healthcare industry is also experiencing new tools taking live thanks to the new possibilities of interaction and exchange that the web provides.

The MeSH (Medical Subject Headings), a comprehensive vocabulary that serves as an index of topics on the life sciences, includes eHealth among the following terms: Telemedicine, Mobile Health, Telehealth, mHealth and Ubiquitous Healthcare (uHealth).

Several systematic reviews of published definitions were analysed to depict a clear articulation of the term. In general, the proposed definitions have considered eHealth the use of information and communication technologies for health applications (Healy 2007). However, the concept varies by the context and the institutions in which it is used (Lewis 2015) and is still not mature in all the health-related disciplines (Dwairej et al. 2016). In addition, eHealth is not limited to the health domain but is used in many disciplines, such as education, insurance and business (Cashen et al. 2004).

Rodrigues et al. (2016) asserts that the term eHealth technologies are tools created to improve the health process. The possible outcome is a new, efficient, equitable way to improve accessibility to health services, which reduces response times, ensures cost savings and offers the possibility of deploying alerts and, ultimately, improving therapeutic and diagnostic efficacy.

eHealth is viewed as the application of ICTs to healthcare, but these terms have a multidisciplinary nature (Jadad et al. 2005). As regards the business nature of the eHealth definitions—which is particularly relevant to this work—Jadad et al. (2005) highlighted that only 11 of the 51 definitions (21%) referred explicitly to the commercial aspects of eHealth. In addition, in Eysenbach's (2001) study, only 6 of 36 definitions (16%) refer to business or e-business. Nevertheless, to achieve the aims of the present study, the discussion will commence from the first Eysenbach (2001) definition that includes the business topic.

Therefore, eHealth can be defined as an emerging field located at the intersection of ICTs, health and business management, referring to the organisation and delivery of health services and information using the Internet and related technologies. In a broader sense, the term characterises not only a technical development but also a new way of working, an attitude and a commitment to networked, global thinking, to improve healthcare locally, regionally and worldwide by using ICTs (Eysenbach 2001).

This extended definition came into use when the eHealth discussion commenced (1999–2000) and served as a 'buzzword' for industry leaders and marketing people interested in exploiting the excitement around other terms, such as e-commerce (Oh et al. 2005).

Evidently, there is a strong mutual relationship between the business approach and eHealth (Hanseth and Bygstad 2015). The more reciprocal the relation, the more the expected benefits of eHealth applications that can be exploited. Next, we discuss the potential benefits of eHealth in detail.

From a managerial perspective, eHealth is viewed in a positive way and represents the promise of ICTs to improve health and healthcare systems (Jadad et al. 2005). The aim of many institutional stakeholders is to exploit and maximise their expected benefits, such as use of innovative technologies to engage with consumers and improve the patient experience (Morris 2019).

The European Union defines the following as the most relevant benefits of the eHealth policies: increased access to personal health data; increased sustainability, efficiency, efficacy and quality of treatment of health system; and empowered healthcare workers and empowered patients (Barbabella et al. 2017).

Noar and Harrington (2012) clarify these expected benefits by presenting more specific advantages. They summarise the advantages for customers (e.g. anonymity) as well as healthcare systems (e.g. automated data collection). These twin perspectives can be considered too simplistic to describe the health services. The eHealth ecosystem includes health and non-health stakeholder's groups. Making the effort to explore their interests and values will help in forming an eHealth solution in terms of the expected benefits that can be delivered to each stakeholder, considering that many studies discuss the benefits of eHealth (Dwairej et al. 2016).

The WHO categorised the stakeholder groups from the health sector (e.g. patients, physicians and healthcare authorities) and the non-health sectors (e.g. investment funds). Each group has different interests, opportunities and challenges. While many stakeholders are part of the WHO's current macro systems, new tech titans, such as Amazon, Google, Microsoft and Apple, have already explored healthcare ecosystems and have developed various aggressive strategies, mostly through partnerships (Engelen et al. 2018). For instance, the biggest health study was conducted by Stanford Medicine together with Apple, with the help of more than 400,000 Apple Watch users who consented to participate in this study (Petersen 2018).

Undoubtedly, if the number of stakeholders is high, a complex phase of identification, engagement and integration of each category's interests is essential. This preliminary phase is paramount to developing a proper eHealth strategy in terms of alignment of expected and actual benefits. It is important to design various scenarios and consider different strategies for each. Many studies have confirmed the multidisciplinary nature of eHealth as well as the necessity to evaluate the eHealth phenomenon. Yamamoto et al. (2019) state that it is necessary to analyse the interrelationships of stakeholders, such as patients, doctors and service providers, to ensure the success of eHealth services and conducting such an analysis is considered one of the main challenges in eHealth implementation.

As regards the services and applications component, Rodrigues et al. (2016) and Black (2011) identify the most relevant applications that have been put into practice. The latter categorised eHealth technologies into four main areas:

Data storage, management and retrieval activities
Support of clinical decision-making
Facilitation of care from a distance
Promotion of health, well-being and digital participation

Data storage, *management* and *retrieval activities* can be considered a series of processes to update the health data of patient. These processes can be deployed by health workers or the patient in paper form or through computerised tools. Rodrigues et al. (2016) identifies the main problems related to the use of paper, such as lack of uniformity, illegibility of certain information and technical difficulties in ensuring the anonymisation of the patient. These issues are easy to solve with an electronic health record (EHR) system, which can also support health professionals to share documents between themselves.

The process of implementing EHR tools has already started. It is worth considering two distinctions. The current generations of systems are called electronic medical records and are proprietary systems designed by a specific organisation. However, the EHRs are systems that usually work beyond proprietary information and facilitate easier data sharing by following a predefined standard. This would mean that a new open and interoperated ecosystem needs standardisation of information systems.

The adoption of a standard is crucial in ensuring interoperability and usually follows a typical dynamic of implementing a new emergent standard and subsequently stabilising it. One such standard, the Health Level 7, is used in the in-hospital communication. In addition, standardisation has a key role in the *picture archiving and communication systems*, the so-called PACS.

Further, considerable attention is devoted to the *Personal Electronic Health Records*, which are managed by patients and linked with their physicians. The empowerment of individual patients may be a turning point of the entire healthcare approach. As Greenhalgh et al. (2010) explain, PHRs are seen as having a key role in the new care model and are an integral part of a wider care package that may reduce clinician workload and overall healthcare costs. During their studies on 'HealthSpace' (Greenhalgh et al. 2010), a digital project on the United Kingdom's NHS, they revealed the risks of abandoning or neglecting these platforms apart from the low adoption rate. The topic is discussed in depth in the next paragraph.

Support of clinical decision-making is considered the second activity that can be improved by eHealth systems. *Computerised provider (or physician) order entry or management* (CPOE) can be integrated within EHRs or provided as standalone modules.

Physicians' orders can be managed by using a CPOE system, and the results (e.g. a PACS image from a radiology laboratory) can be delivered in the same way. CPOE can be implemented along with an *ePrescribing interface*. The explicit purpose of such a system is facilitating communication between the prescriber and the pharmacy. Predictably, studies reveal that new stakeholders should be well integrated into these new systems.

Computerised decision support systems should improve clinical decision-making as regards various care activities and their related processes. Allowing practitioners to make clinical decisions that comply with the relevant guidelines can be considered an appropriate example of such improvements

Moving from the most recent applications to the well-structured and most known technologies, the classification highlighted the concept of *Telemedicine*, a term coined in the 1970s. For the purpose of this thesis, it is assumed that other terms, such as telesurgery and telemonitoring, or other clinical applications (e.g. telecardiology) should be identified as parts of Telemedicine.

The WHO defines Telemedicine as ‘the delivery of healthcare services, where distance is a critical factor, by all health care professionals using information and communication technologies for the exchange of valid information for diagnosis, treatment and prevention of disease and injuries, research and evaluation, and for the continuing education of health care providers, all in the interests of advancing the health of individuals and their communities’ (Chen and Dart 2019). In other words, it can be provided using different types of ICTs, both analogical (e.g. television health and basic voice telephony) and digital. Regarding the difference from eHealth, both the terms refer to the use of ICTs in the healthcare field. Even so, eHealth definitions present the exclusive application of the ‘Internet or related technologies’ (Eysenbach 2001) and a more general approach to improve health services. There is disagreement about the comprehensiveness of the eHealth and Telemedicine concepts and whether eHealth is the umbrella term that includes Telemedicine or vice versa. However, it seems to be clear that Telemedicine involves the ICTs primarily to deliver clinical services and remains linked to medical professionals, whereas eHealth also provides non-clinical healthcare services driven by the patients (Dwairej et al. 2016).

The third of aim is *facilitating care from a distance*. Two commonly used technologies are considered a part of this category: Telehealth and telecare. Telehealth applications enable the remote exchange of physiological data between the medical staff and patients to assist in monitoring. Investing in Telehealth may expand outpatient services while also helping hospitals to reduce costs and boost revenue (Holden et al. 2019).

Telecare is related to keeping people safe in their homes using remotely accessed technologies. Traditionally, telecare applications are alarms and sensors (e.g. call alarm buttons). A wireless sensor network for monitoring people, a wireless body area network and ambient assisted living are the principal topics of this work. The Internet of Things ‘makes smart objectives the ultimate building blocks in the development of cyber-physical smart pervasive frameworks’ (Islam et al. 2015). As an example, during the past decade, wearable devices, smart electronic devices (an electronic device with microcontrollers) that can be incorporated into clothing or worn on the body as implants or accessories, have been used in various fields, such as sports, consumer applications, lifestyle and fitness products and healthcare (Haghi et al. 2017). The smart wearable market is expected to register a compound annual growth rate[2] (CAGR) of 19.10% in 2019–2024 (Aitken and Lyle 2015). Importantly, nearly 90% of consumer wearables synchronise wirelessly with an app, usually through a mobile phone, to provide users access to data (Aitken and Lyle 2015).

Following this trend, it is essential to open the discussion on Mobile Health (mHealth). This term refers to the utilisation of mobile devices, in particular, smartphones, in the healthcare field. Fiordelli et al. (2013) revealed a series of mHealth interventions directed most frequently at self-management and a field that is becoming more structured, coherent and solid. Certainly, mHealth is historically a part of the eHealth concept, and it is considered one of its sub-segments (Dwairej et al. 2016). Nevertheless, during the past decade (2008–2018), the number of articles in the peer-reviewed scientific literature has dramatically increased, which reveals the strong interest in this topic. Moreover, the *Journal of Medical Internet Research*, which is, according to the Journal Impact Factor 2017, the leader of digital health and medical informatics journals, presents since 2012 a dedicated publication termed *JMIR mHealth and uHealth*.

Many studies have revealed the increase in health mobile apps in addition to the increasing interest and excitement regarding mHealth management (Aitken and Lyle 2015; Cobelli and Chiarini (2020). Moreover, the global mHealth market is expected to grow from US$52.6 billion in 2019 to US$332.7 billion in 2025 (Fiordelli et al. 2013).

The concept of mHealth is also related to the second topic that is presented in the table: uHealth. *Ubiquitous Healthcare* has been developed from the 5-A model: Any data, Any device, Any network, Anytime and Anywhere. The uHealth system is a comprehensive solution to patient-centred healthcare and usually makes use of mobile devices. In fact, this wide concept is practically implemented in a system that has three components: a device that receives signals from the patient, a smartphone app or a device that transmits the acquired signals to a server, which monitors and analyses the signals with lifelog data (Kim et al. 2018). The lifelog data contain a dataset of each patient's activities and life.

In addition to these activities, medical services perform other tasks, such as the *promotion of health, well-being and digital participation*. It is considered a broad concept that has various effects on numerous disciplines. According to Lewin et al. (2010), these services, for instance, can be 'delivered to educate and stimulate social interaction so as to enrich the lives of older and disabled people who live at home'.

Lastly, certain new technologies are available that have possible applications in the eHealth field, such as avatars and virtual representation of the self, bots and virtual reality. Some of these solutions may be considered complementarities of current eHealth systems to solve their intrinsic issues. For instance, virtual reality technology is transforming the process of medical training by creating realistic scenarios for physicians (e.g. the Surgical Theater company provides a preoperation

[2] The term CAGR is used by investments advisors to indicate their market knowledge and by funds to promote their returns.

rehearsal platform for complex surgeries) (Mazurek et al. 2019). Artificial intelligence or robotics can transform healthcare delivery, providing decision support and practitioner assistance for tasks such as diagnosing patients and spotting disease outbreaks earlier and accelerating the development of new drugs and devices (Morris 2019).

The aforementioned general and digital trends have strong effects on healthcare delivery. As revealed by previous studies, the complex dynamics of healthcare could reshape the health systems in the near future to solve the current healthcare problems. In addition, it is noted that a chasm exists between the types of care and support that patients receive and what they should have and calls for fundamental change in healthcare systems, which would be more beneficial to patients and clinician (Fernandopulle et al. 2003).

Many studies have discussed the future structure and organisation of healthcare delivery. For instance, Ferguson (1995) defined the healthcare shift from an *industrial age* to an *information age*. In the industrial age, the concept of self-care is not considered, and the delivery system is predetermined in primary, secondary and tertiary care based on a disease-focused model. Conversely, in the information age, patients' involvement in their care is viewed by some as both inherently desirable (empowering) and potentially cost saving. Moreover, patients and caregivers appear to be demanding change, dissatisfied with poor services and lack of transparency (Carlson and Greeley 2010). The patient is viewed as an active partner through self-care management (Greenhalgh et al. 2010). Similar to other researchers, Ferguson shows the importance of ICTs in the new healthcare delivery. For instance, Charmel and Frampton (2008) affirm that ICTs could drive the current healthcare systems to the patient-centred care that has the potential to reduce adverse events, malpractice claims and operating costs. They define patient-centred care as 'a healthcare setting in which patients are encouraged to be actively involved in their care, with a physical environment that promotes patient comfort and staff who are dedicated to meeting the physical, emotional and spiritual needs of the patients' (Charmel and Frampton 2008).

Moreover, Koop et al. (2008) focus on the process of decentralisation of healthcare delivery from hospitals, which have centralised providers, knowledge and specialists, to a distributed healthcare network by bridging technology directly into the home or to the local clinics. In their view, the hospitals may retain specialised services, trauma care, transplantation or oncology. The idea of decentralisation could affect the physician–patient relationship. For instance, both can contribute actively to the collection of patient records (Delbanco et al. 2001). The healthcare complexity due to increasing legislation and severe budget cuts is creating an administrative burden for professionals that distract them from delivering actual care (Friedberg et al. 2014). Supporting patient contribution may be a solution to this problem. Regardless, ICTs can support the transition from institution-centric to patient-centric applications to promote disease management and prevention (Demiris 2016).

The patient care model and the decentralisation process seem to be part of the same shift to a new way of healthcare delivery. This new paradigm is not merely philosophical; in fact, many studies discuss its practical application that includes eight main dimensions (Lauver et al. 2002): (1) respect for the patient's values, preferences and expressed needs; (2) information and education (patient engagement in care); (3) superb access to care (e.g. ease of making an appointment, short waiting time and efficient use of physicians' time); (4) emotional support to relieve fear and anxiety; (5) involvement of friends and family; (6) physical comfort; (7) continuity and secure transition between healthcare settings; and (8) coordination of care (e.g. prompt feedback of specialist consultation reports to primary care physicians and patients or post-hospital follow-up and support).

In such a scenario, in this study we investigate the behaviour of healthcare professionals who own or manage a community-based private practice.

If it is true that in future, healthcare delivery will involve dealing with a paradigm shift, from a managerial point of view, the extent to which professionals intend to adopt new technological tools is unclear. No innovation in the current healthcare systems can be promoted without the intent of individuals to actively participate in changing the process and to engage in healthcare processes and decisions (Demiris 2016).

Simultaneously, the current institution-centric healthcare organisation would become more decentralised, as Koop et al. (2008) indicate. A process of delocalisation could occur—from hospital to home/car to everywhere or from physician to patients in a wider environment—by which public organisations, as hospitals, and community-based private practices can work together through the support of new information technology tools. In other words, healthcare, under the influence of ICTs, is progressing from centralised institutional care to a networked system. In this sense, new technologies can rapidly change patients' requirements as well as their expectations.

The empowerment of patients and their wish for community-based services are also determined by several practices that are becoming increasingly relevant in their view.

As the health industry evolves, creative healthcare business model generation is determining results in the market. Some healthcare business ideas are healthcare industry business models and solutions, including value-based care models, new payment paradigms and decentralised healthcare.

Decentralisation is vital in this scenario, and traditional and new businesses are adapting their models to better meet patients' needs and expectations. The existence of these private businesses is also related to the economic and logistic limits of NHSs to keep pace with innovative services and products available for patients.

What is clear is that all these community-based private practices have a business model in common. They operate within the healthcare system but have the private structure typical of a retailer, eventually with mutual agreements with the NHSs. Their product and services are not provided directly through the NHS, but they are essential, for NHSs as well as for patients.

These specific practices are those we are interested in investigating to understand the behaviour of their owners/managers and, precisely, their attitude towards new and innovative technologies that we will define in the context of eHealth.

References

Adams R, Bessant J, Phelps R (2006) Innovation management measurement: A review. Int J Manag Rev 8(1):21–47
Aitken M, Lyle J (2015) Patient adoption of mHealth: use, evidence and remaining barriers to mainstream acceptance. IMS Institute for Healthcare Informatics, Parsippany
Al-Fuqaha A, Guizani M, Mohammadi M et al (2015) Internet of things: A survey on enabling technologies, protocols, and applications. IEEE Commun Sur Tutor 17(4):2347–2376
Annarumma C, Palumbo R, Cavallone M (2017) Who empowers whom? The role of organizational health literacy in empowering patients. Sinergie Ital J Manag 104Sep–Dec:11-27
Balachandra R, Friar JH (1997) Factors for success in R&D projects and new product innovation: a contextual framework. IEEE Trans Eng Manag 44(3):276–287
Barbabella F, Melchiorre MG, Quattrini S et al (2017) How can eHealth improve care for people with multimorbidity in Europe? World Health Organization, Berlin
Benkaouz Y, Erradi M (2015) A distributed protocol for privacy preserving aggregation with non-permanent participants. Computing 97(9):893–912
Black A, Car J, Pagliari C et al (2011) The impact of eHealth on the quality and safety of health care: a systematic overview. PLoS Med 8:e1000387
Blobel B, Engelbrecht R, Shifrin MA (eds) (2012) Large scale projects in eHealth: partnership in modernization. IOS Press, Amsterdam
Brian K (2015) OECD insights. Income inequality: the gap between rich and poor. OECD, Paris
Brown MT, Bussell J, Dutta S et al (2016) Medication adherence: truth and consequences. Am J Med Sci 351(4):387–399
Bukh PN, Nielsen C (2010) Understanding the health care business model: the financial analyst's point of view. J Health Care Finance 37(2):8–26
Carlson G, Greeley H (2010) Is the relationship between your hospital and your medical staff sustainable? J Healthc Manag 55(3):158–173
Cashen MS, Dykes P, Gerber B (2004) eHealth technology and Internet resources: barriers for vulnerable populations. J Cardiovasc Nurs 19(3):209–214
Cavicchi C, Vagnoni E (2017) Does intellectual capital promote the shift of healthcare organizations towards sustainable development? Evidence from Italy. J Clean Prod 153:275–286
Charmel PA, Frampton SB (2008) Building the business case for patient-centered care. Healthc Financial Manag 62(3):80–85
Chen LW, Dart B (2019) A renewed framework for local health departments. J Public Health Manag Pract 25(1):5–6
Cobelli N, Chiarini A (2020) Improving customer satisfaction and loyalty through mHealth service digitalization: new challenges for Italian pharmacists. TQM J. https://doi.org/10.1108/TQM-10-2019-0252. (In Press)
Cooper RG (1979) The dimensions of industrial new product success and failure. J Mark 43(3):93–103
Cordero R (1990) The measurement of innovation performance in the firm: an overview. Res Policy 19(2):185–192
De Belvis AG, Ferrè F, Specchia ML et al (2012) The financial crisis in Italy: implications for the healthcare sector. Health Policy 106(1):10–16
De Brentani U (1991) Success factors in developing new business services. Eur J Mark 25(2):33–59
Delbanco T, Berwick DM, Boufford JI et al (2001) Healthcare in a land called PeoplePower: nothing about me without me. Health Expect 4(3):144–150
Demiris G (2016) Consumer health informatics: past, present, and future of a rapidly evolving domain. Yearb Med Inform 25(S 01):S42–S47
Dwairej D, Massadeh A, Enab E et al (2016) E-health concept development and maturity in literature. J Health Med Nurs 29:156–166
Dzau VJ, Yoediono Z, ElLaissi WF et al (2013) Fostering innovation in medicine and health care: what must academic health centers do? Acad Med 88(10):1424–1429

Ellner AL, Stout S, Sullivan EE et al (2015) Health systems innovation at academic health centers: leading in a new era of health care delivery. Acad Med 90(7):872–880
Engelen L, Jacobs F, Hulsebosch M (2018) Augmented health (care)(tm): the end of the beginning. Lucien Engelen Holding Bv
Ernst H (2002) Success factors of new product development: a review of the empirical literature. Int J Manag Rev 4(1):1–40
Eysenbach G (2001) What is e-health? J Med Internet Res 3(2):1–2
Fatehi F, Wootton R (2012) Telemedicine, telehealth or e-health? A bibliometric analysis of the trends in the use of these terms. J Telemed Telecare 18(8):460–464
Ferguson T (1995) Consumer health informatics. Healthc Forum J 38(1):28
Fernandopulle R, Ferris T, Epstein A et al (2003) A research agenda for bridging the 'quality chasm'. Health Aff 22(2):178–190
Fiordelli M, Diviani N, Schulz PJ (2013) Mapping mHealth research: a decade of evolution. J Med Internet Res 15(5):1–15
Freed J, Lowe C, Flodgren G et al (2018) Telemedicine: is it really worth it? A perspective from evidence and experience. BMJ Health Care Inform 25(1):14–18
Frenkel A, Maital S, Grupp H (2000) Measuring dynamic technical change: a technometric approach. Int J Tech Manag 20(3):429–441
Friedberg MW, Chen PG, Van Busum KR et al (2014) Factors affecting physician professional satisfaction and their implications for patient care, health systems, and health policy. Rand Health Quart *3*(4):1
Gaddi A, Capello F, Manca M (eds) (2013) eHealth, care and quality of life. Springer Science & Business Media, Berlin
George C, Whitehouse D, Duquenoy P (eds) (2012) eHealth: legal, ethical and governance challenges. Springer Science & Business Media, New York
Gibbons MC (ed) (2007) eHealth solutions for healthcare disparities. Springer Science & Business Media, New York
Gibbons MC, Shaikh Y (2019) Introduction to consumer health informatics and digital inclusion. In: Edmunds M, Hass C, Holve E (eds) Consumer informatics and digital health. Springer, New York, pp 25–41
Globe S, Levy GW, Schwartz CM (1973) Key factors and events in the innovation process. Res Management 16(4):8–15
Greenhalgh T, Hinder S, Stramer K et al (2010) Adoption, non-adoption, and abandonment of a personal electronic health record: case study of HealthSpace. BMJ 341:1–11
Griffin A (1997) The effect of project and process characteristics on product development cycle time. J Mark Res 34(1):24–35
Hagberg J, Sundstrom M, Egels-Zandén N (2016) The digitalization of retailing: an exploratory framework. Int J Retail Distrib Manag 44(7):694–712
Haghi M, Thurow K, Stoll R (2017) Wearable devices in medical internet of things: scientific research and commercially available devices. Healthc Inform Res 23(1):4–15
Hanseth O, Bygstad B (2015) Flexible generification: ICT standardization strategies and service innovation in health care. Eur J Inform Syst 24(6):645–663
Healy JC (2007) The WHO eHealth Resolution. Methods Inf Med 46(01):02–04
Hernandez LM (ed) (2009) Health literacy, eHealth, and communication: putting the consumer first: workshop summary. National Academies Press, Washington
Hillman KM, Athari F, Frost SA, Braithwaite J (2018) The silver tsunami: the impact of the aging population on healthcare. In: Braithwaite J, Mannion R, Matsuyama Y et al (eds) Healthcare systems: future predictions for global care. CRC Press, USA, pp 367–372
Ho K, Jarvis-Selinger S, Lauscher HN et al (eds) (2012) Technology enabled knowledge translation for eHealth: principles and practice. Springer Science & Business Media, New York
Holden KB, Hopkins J, Belton A et al (2019) Leveraging science to advance health equity: a regional health policy research center's approach. Ethn Dis 29(Suppl 2):323–328

Hörbst A, Hayn D, Schreier G (eds) (2014) EHealth2014–health informatics meets eHealth: outcomes research: the benefit of health-IT, vol 198. IOS Press, Amsterdam
Islam SR, Kwak D, Kabir MH et al (2015) The internet of things for health care: a comprehensive survey. IEEE Access 3:678–708
Italian National Statistics Institute, Il sistema dei conti della sanità per l'Italia (years 2014–16), 2017. Available at https://www.istat.it/. Accessed 16 Dec 2019
Jadad A, Oh H, Rizo C et al (2005) What eHealth: a systematic review of published definitions. J Med Internet Res 7(1):1–12
Kim S, Yeom S, Kwon OJ et al (2018) Ubiquitous healthcare system for analysis of chronic patients' biological and lifelog data. IEEE Access 6:8909–8915
Kodama M (ed) (2015) Collaborative innovation: developing health support ecosystems. Routledge, London
Koop CE, Mosher R, Kun L et al (2008) Future delivery of health care: cybercare. IEEE Eng Med Biol Mag 27(6):29–38
Lauver DR, Ward SE, Heidrich SM et al (2002) Patient-centered interventions. Res Nurs Health 25(4):246–255
Lavalle T, Omosebi CD, Desmarteau RH (2015) The dynamics of social capital and health. Acta Bio Medica Atenei Parmensis 86(3 Suppl):223–232
Lavoie-Tremblay M, Aubry M, Cyr G et al (2017) Innovation in health service management: adoption of project management offices to support major health care transformation. J Nurs Manag 25(8):657–665
Lewin D, Adshead S, Glennon B et al (2010) Assisted living technologies for older and disabled people in 2030. Final report. Plum Consulting, 1–72
Lewis LM (2015) The promise and ambiguity of eHealth research. Nurs Res 64(3):157–158
Liao Y, Deschamps F, Loures EDFR et al (2017) Past, present and future of Industry 4.0: a systematic literature review and research agenda proposal. Int J Prod Res 55(12):3609–3629
Lipworth W, Axler R (2016) Towards a bioethics of innovation. J Med Ethics 42(7):445–449
Lister C, Payne H, Hanson CL et al (2017) The public health innovation model: merging private sector processes with public health strengths. Front Public Health 5:192
Marmor TR (2013) Health care politics and policy: the business of medicine: A course for physician leaders. Yale J Biol Med 86(3):407–411
Mazurek J, Kiper P, Cieślik B et al (2019) Virtual reality in medicine: a brief overview and future research directions. Hum Mov 20(3):16–22
Meier CA, Fitzgerald MC, Smith JM (2013) eHealth: extending, enhancing, and evolving health care. Annu Rev Biom Eng 15:59–382
Menvielle L, Audrain-Pontevia AF, Menvielle W (eds) (2017) The digitization of healthcare: new challenges and opportunities. Springer, New York
Miller FA, French M (2016) Organizing the entrepreneurial hospital: hybridizing the logics of healthcare and innovation. Res Pol 45(8):1534–1544
Ministry of Economic Development (n.d.), Italy's National Plan Impresa 4.0. Available via https://www.mise.gov.it. Accessed 22 Dec 2019
Morris M (2019) Global health care outlook. Making progress against persistent challenges. Deloitte, London
Noar SM, Harrington NG (eds) (2012) eHealth applications: promising strategies for behavior change. Routledge, London
Oh H, Rizo C, Enkin M et al (2005) What is eHealth: a systematic review of published definitions. World Hosp Health Serv 41(1):31–49
Parviainen P, Tihinen M, Kääriäinen J, Teppola S (2017) Tackling the digitalization challenge: how to benefit from digitalization in practice. Int J Inf Syst Proj Manag 5(1):63–77
Perelman J (2017) Evolution and patterns of global health financing 1995–2014. Lancet 389(10083):1981–2004
Petersen A (2018) Digital health and technological promise: a sociological inquiry. Routledge, London

Porter ME, Ketels CH (2003) UK Competitiveness: moving to the next stage. Economic and Social Research Council, London
Rodrigues J, Compte SS, Díez I (2016) e-Health systems: theory and technical applications. Elsevier, Amsterdam
Rosenmöller M, Whitehouse D, Wilson P (eds) (2014) Managing eHealth: from vision to reality. Springer, New York
Rothwell R (1992) Successful industrial innovation: critical factors for the 1990s. R&D Manag 22(3):221–240
Shimizu T, Eto R, Horiguchi I et al (2005) Relationship between turnover and periodic health check-up data among Japanese hospital nurses: a three-year follow-up study. J Occup Health 47(4):327–333
Showell C, Nohr C (2012) How should we define eHealth, and does the definition matter? Qual Life Through Qual Inf 180:881–884
Snowdon AW, Bassi H, Scarffe AD, Smith AD (2015) Reverse innovation: an opportunity for strengthening health systems. Glob Health 11(1):1–7
Tamblyn R, McMahon M, Nadigel J et al (2016) Health system transformation through research innovation. Healthc Pap 16(Special Issue):8–19
Tan J (ed) (2005) E-health care information systems: an introduction for students and professionals. Wiley-Blackwell, NJ
Thuemmler C, Bai C (2017) Health 4.0: how virtualization and big data are revolutionizing healthcare. Springer, New York
Vitalari NP (2016) Prospects for the future of the US healthcare industry: a speculative analysis. Am J Med Res 3(2):7–52
West MA, Farr JL (1990) Innovation at work. In: West MA, Farr JL (eds) Innovation and creativity at work: psychological and organizational strategies. Wiley, Chichester
White L, Klinner C, Cobelli N (2011) Improving the uptake of the Australian Home Medicines Review (AHMR) through patient segmentation. Int J Pharm Healthc Mark 5(3):194–204
World Health Organization (2018) Public spending on health: a closer look at global trends (No. WHO/HIS/HGF/HF Working Paper/18.3). WHO, Geneva
Yamamoto S, Olayan NI, Morisaki S (2019) Analyzing e-Health business models using actor relationship matrix. Acta Sci Med Sci 3(3):105–111

Chapter 2
The Choices of Adoption of eHealth Tools: An Analysis of Research Models

Abstract Many studies have demonstrated that, in general, the adoption of eHealth systems is often problematic. The starting point is the large mismatch between the potential and the empirically demonstrated benefits of eHealth applications. Moreover, the cost-effectiveness and the risk of implementing these solutions are not always clear. In addition, the scepticism of healthcare professionals regarding the actual benefits it would offer their patients and them is frequently a barrier in the eHealth system adoption process. The many interconnected and complex issues related to the nature of healthcare systems' transformation can be defined as a set of persistent problems. These issues are usually the outcomes of poor models of innovation diffusion. Indeed, the existing healthcare systems tend to create more obstacles to innovation compared with systems in other industries. Moreover, the healthcare systems, thus far, have demonstrated a low rate of information technology appropriation. In this chapter, we will describe several research models developed to comprehend and evaluate the choices of adoption/non-adoption of new technologies to provide entrepreneurs and managers of community-based private practices certain insights and tools to understand the ways in which eHealth can be helpful and beneficial for all healthcare system stakeholders.

Keywords eHealth adoption · TRA · Research models · Innovation choices

2.1 A Preliminary Overview of eHealth Adoption Measurements

The previous chapter describes the main challenges of healthcare systems and the related causes and effects on different typologies of such systems. In this regard, rapid technological change challenges established business models and simultaneously provides opportunities for adopting new technologies (Lai 2017), and business organisations often seek to shape the evolution of technological applications to their own advantage.

N. Cobelli, *Innovation in Community-Based Private Practices Through eHealth*, International Series in Advanced Management Studies,
https://doi.org/10.1007/978-3-030-48177-3_2

To cover the scope of the present research, a fundamental requirement is having a clear view on innovation dynamics for understanding the complexity of choices before, during and after new technology adoption.

To this end, a literary review was conducted on the main models, and the factors determining the choices of innovation adoption/non-adoption were investigated. Therefore, this chapter presents a literature review of the Technology Acceptance Models and the theories leading to the development of novel technology.

Section 2.2 will focus on the main interdisciplinary models aimed at understanding the reasons behind the choices of adoption/non-adoption of an innovation. Further, interdisciplinary contributions on the choice factors observed in a perspective closer to that which animates this volume will be particularly focused on. Specifically, in Sect. 2.2, reference will be made to research models more pertinent to the social sciences and widely used in sociological, psychological and business management research.

This literature review is particularly relevant in this research, since it provides scientific tools to investigate the attitudes and behaviours of potential users and constitutes the basis for the empirical study presented in Chap. 3.

2.2 Research Models About the Choices of Innovation Adoption/Non-adoption

Over the past 30 years, the field of interdisciplinary study of innovation adoption has developed rapidly. Different theoretical models were developed and applied. The result of these many years of research is the numerous contributions to the field, which, however, remain highly fragmented. Since the 1960s, researchers in various disciplines have published many studies about adoption of technologies by individuals (Ogrezeanu 2015). In Table 2.1, the timeline of the main research models under discussion in this research is presented.

In 1980, Ajzen and Fishbein introduced the Theory of Reasoned Action (TRA), a social–psychological theory that has a rather wide area of applicability to many areas of human behaviour. TRA is among the most basic and influential theories on human behaviour. It attempts to explain human behaviours that are intentional and reasoned as opposed to spontaneous or emotional.

It is the first theory to establish a link between intention and behaviours, and it proposes that behaviours are generally determined by the behavioural intention of subjects (Ajzen and Fishbein 1980).

In other words, the researchers explain the concept of 'attitude' as the individual's evaluation of an object and 'belief' as the link between an object and some attribute. In addition, they define 'behaviour' as a result or intention, as described in Fig. 2.1. Attitudes are affective and based on a set of beliefs about the object of behaviour or an individual's positive or negative feelings (evaluative affect) about performing the target behaviour (Ajzen and Fishbein 1980). A second factor is the social standards of individuals' perceptions of the attitude of their immediate community to certain activities or their perception that most people who are important

Table 2.1 The main models studying the choices of adoption/non-adoption of innovation

Year	Research models	Core constructs
1980	Theory of Reasoned Action (TRA)	Attitude, subjective norm
1985 and 1991	Theory of Planned Behaviour (TPB)	Attitude, subjective norm, perceived behavioural control
1986 and 2002	Matching Person and Technology (MPT) model	Environment, person, technology functionality
1989	Technology Acceptance Model (TAM)	Perceived usefulness, perceived ease of use, subjective norm/external variables
1992	Motivational Model (MM)	Extrinsic motivation, intrinsic motivation
	Innovation Diffusion Theory (IDT)	Five perceived attributes
1995	Task–Technology Fit (TTF) model	Task requirement, tool functionalities
	Social Cognitive Theory (SCT)	Self-efficacy, affect, anxiety, outcome expectations
2000	Technology Acceptance Model (TAM 2)	Social influence, cognitive instrumental processes
2003	Unified Theory of Acceptance and Use of Technology (UTAUT)	Performance expectancy, effort expectancy, social influence, facilitating conditions, gender, age, experience, voluntariness of use
2008	Technology Acceptance Model (TAM 3)	Pre- and post-implementation phases

Source: Author's elaboration

Table 2.1 chronologically lists the main research models that investigate the choices of adoption/non-adoption of innovation

to them think they should or should not perform the behaviour in question. The determinant attitudes and subjective norms are broadly specified in TRA since it is conceived as a broad theory of human behaviour. TRA has been applied in the psychological studies of many behaviours, from consumer to health behaviours.

In 1985, Ajzen developed the Theory of Planned Behaviour (TPB), which states that individuals' behavioural intentions and behaviours are determined by their subjective norms, behavioural control and attitude towards behaviours. Ajzen presents a review of several studies using TPB to predict intentions and behaviours in a wide range of settings (see Fig. 2.2). In general, TPB extends TRA by adding the construct of perceived behavioural control (Venkatesh and Davis 2000). Attitude and subjective norms are the same factors as in the TRA model. The third factor, defined as perceived behavioural control, is the control users perceive that may limit their behaviour.

TPB is focused on studying the inconsistent association between behavioural intentions and actual behaviours as regards long-term expected behaviours.

Often, therefore, individuals may have the intention to perform certain behaviours, but such behaviours fail to materialise or cease before their effects can be achieved. This may be the case either because individuals change their minds about

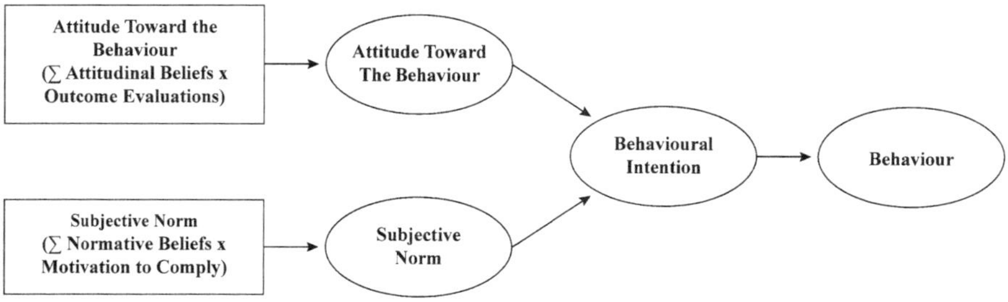

Fig. 2.1 The Theory of Reasoned Action (TRA) model. Figure 2.1 represents the TRA model, which aims to explain the relationship between attitudes and behaviours in human action. It is mainly used to predict individuals' behaviours based on their pre-existing attitudes and behavioural intentions. An individual's decision to engage in a particular behaviour is based on the outcomes that the individual expects will occur as a result of performing the behaviour (source: Ajzen and Fishbein 1980)

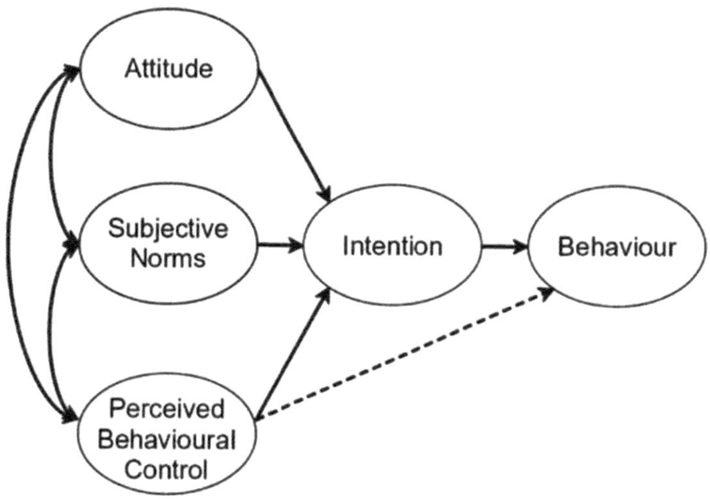

Fig. 2.2 The Theory of Planned Behaviour (TPB) model. Figure 2.2 shows the TPB model, which states that the intention towards behaviour, subjective norms and perceived behavioural control together shape an individual's behavioural intentions and behaviours (source: Ajzen 1985)

the desirability of the behaviour or because they are unable to perform the behaviour. The claim is that the perceived behavioural control influences directly not only the actual behaviour but also the process of forming the intention to perform the behaviour. Once again, it should be mentioned TPB, similar to TRA, is a broad psychological theory about human behaviour, which has been applied and verified in various areas of psychology and in social sciences.

Extensive research has been conducted in the business management field on TRA and on TPB, although such studies mostly focus on products already in the marketplace and include the view of society (Lai 2017).

A related model is the Decomposed Theory of Planned Behaviour (DTPB) model. Unlike TPB, but similar to the Technology Acceptance Model (TAM), DTPB 'decomposes' attitude, subjective norm and perceived behavioural influence into the underlying structure of belief within the context of technological adoption (Venkatesh and Bala 2008).

Further, the Matching Person and Technology (MPT) model discusses three main areas of evaluation: determination of environmental factors affecting use, recognition of user needs and preferences and overview of the functions and characteristics of the most suitable and acceptable technology (Scherer and Craddock 2002). It emerged from the Grounded Theory[1] research and was developed in 1986 by Scherer. Specifically, MPT is based on the research on the use and non-use of recommended assistive technology by consumers with a variety of disabilities (Scherer and Craddock 2002). The MPT process is both a personal and collaborative (i.e. user and provider working together) assessment and consists of a series of paper-and-pencil measures that can also be used as interview guides; it has separate measures for general, assistive, educational, workplace and healthcare technology use (Scherer and Craddock 2002). The MPT model has corresponding evaluation methods used in the selection and decision-making regarding technology as well as the findings of studies on discrepancies between consumers of technology, non-users, avoiders and reticent users.

In 1995, three main theories showed different innovation dynamics: the Innovation Diffusion Theory (IDT), the Task–Technology Fit (TTF) model and the Social Cognitive Theory (SCT).

The concerns of the IDT, a theory proposed by Rogers, are not as broad as that of TPB and TRA that consider all types of human behaviour. IDT is specifically focused on the phenomenon of diffusion, at the social and group level and the behaviour of innovation adoption, usually observed at the individual level. It is a highly complex theory that explicitly or implicitly implies a set of variables that function as determinants of the actions of individuals in adopting new technology (Ogrezeanu 2015).

[1] The Grounded Theory is a general methodology that proposes systematic guidelines for gathering and analysing data to generate middle-range theory. The title 'Grounded Theory' mirrors its fundamental premise that researchers can and should develop theory from rigorous analyses of empirical data. The analytic process consists of coding data; developing, checking and integrating theoretical categories; and writing analytic narratives throughout inquiry. Barney G. Glaser and Anselm L. Strauss (1967), the originators of Grounded Theory, first proposed that researchers should engage in simultaneous data collection and analysis, which has become a routine practice in qualitative research. From the beginning of the research process, the researcher codes the data, compares data and codes and identifies analytic leads and tentative categories to develop through further data collection.

Rogers (2010) defines diffusion as the process by which an innovation is communicated through certain channels over time among the members of a social system. The determinants of the new technology adoption are the innovation as perceived by the potential adopters, the communication channels, the adopters and the social system. This concept is also paramount in the health context. For instance, according to van Gemert-Pijnen et al. (2011), the introduction of eHealth applications requires careful communication among the multitude of stakeholders.

In addition, certain other concepts are useful in achieving the aim of this research. One is the five perceived attributes that Rogers identified, which help in understanding the different rates of adoption of innovations:

- Relative Advantage: the degree to which an innovation is perceived as better than the idea it supersedes
- Compatibility: in the technical sense and with the existing values and needs of the adopters
- Degree of Complexity: the degree to which an innovation is perceived as relatively difficult to understand and use
- Trialability: the degree to which an innovation may be experimented with on a limited basis
- Observability: the degree to which the results of an innovation are visible to others

Moreover, Rogers defines diffusion as a process by which an innovation spreads slowly at first and that eventually reaches saturation level. This dynamic is described by the innovative curve, which presents different groups of adopters throughout the product lifespan: innovators, early adopters, early majority, late majority and laggards (see Fig. 2.3).

With reference to the characteristics of the groups, Geoffrey A. Moore added the idea of the so-called chasm (gap) between early and later adopters. Early adopter categories are qualitatively different from later adopter categories and not just in minor ways as the other categories. Consequently, a successful business model needs to cross the chasm between the 'early market' of tech enthusiasts and visionaries to the mainstream market where customers want solutions and convenience.

Namely, Roger's conclusions can be reported from Oderanti and Li (2018) findings for three companies. Using a sample of people with social care needs who could benefit from long-term use of Telehealth and telecare as the potential population target, they provide insights to these companies on the segments to address next (see Fig. 2.4). They argue that eHealth entrepreneurs need to understand the different attributes of their target groups and the percentage of people who have already adopted the innovation, to structure their products or services.

Indeed, there is another helpful perspective. According to Eysenbach (2005), the eHealth system presents the diffusion of innovation reversed. The author argues that in trials of eHealth interventions, the process starts with an enrolled population of

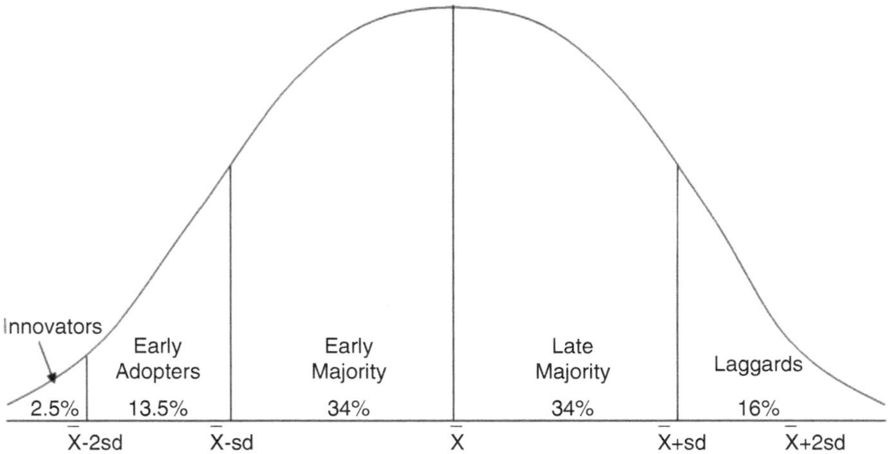

Fig. 2.3 Adopter categorisation on the basis of innovativeness. Figure 2.3 identifies the adopter categories as the classifications of members of a social system on the basis of innovativeness. The categories are innovators, early adopters, early majority, late majority and laggards. In each adopter category, individuals are similar in terms of their innovativeness. The distribution of adopters is a normal distribution (source: Rogers EM (2010) Diffusion of innovations. Simon & Schuster, New York, p. 44)

'intent-to-use' individuals who have already agreed to use the application. However, many individuals discontinue its use and drop out of the trial.

Moreover, Rogers illustrates that little research has been conducted from the reversal of decisions perspective and called for more research on this topic. This contribution distinguishes two typologies of decision: those that lead to rejection owing to dissatisfied individuals and the replacement discontinuance and the adoption of a better idea that replaces the previous one.

Similarly, Eysenbach (2005) discusses dropout attrition, which is the phenomenon of losing participants to follow-up and the phenomenon of non-usage attrition. The author terms this dynamic the law of attrition, the observation that in any eHealth trial a substantial proportion of users drop out before completion or stop using the application and proposes a hypothetical sigmoid attrition curve (see Fig. 2.4).

The curve presents three phases. There is an initial phase where individuals use eHealth solutions out of curiosity. This phase is followed by the attrition (or rejection) stage where people realise the actual benefits of the solution. Lastly, phase three presents a stable user group—hardcore users—continue to utilise the solution.

The attrition curve reveals an initial rapid decrease in the number of participants (Fig. 2.5.).

Moreover, the author states that differential dropout or usage rates between two interventions could be a standard metric for the usability efficacy of a system.

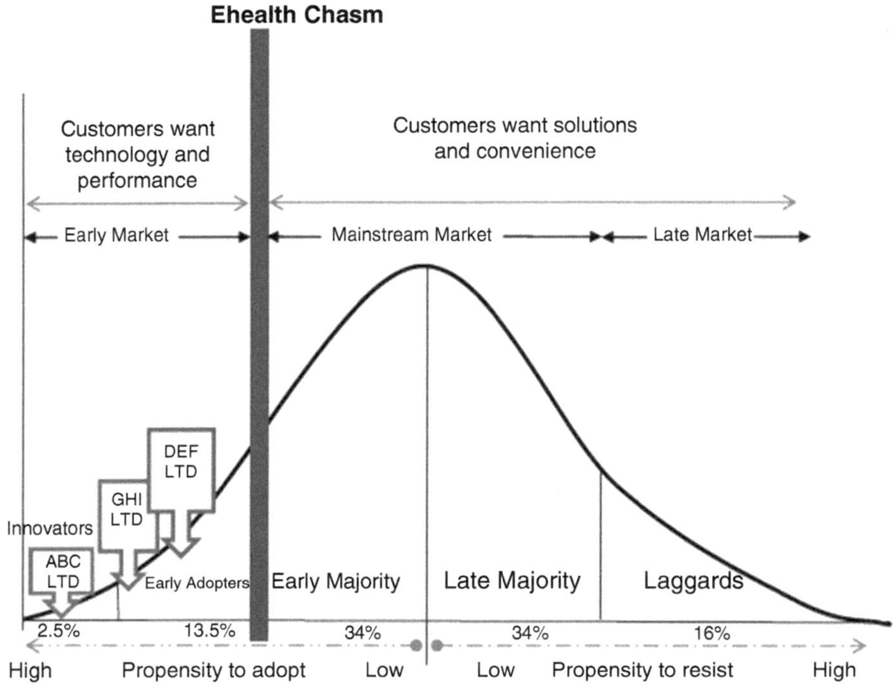

Fig. 2.4 The innovation diffusion curve: eHealth case studies. Figure 2.4 shows the bell curve for the distribution of individual innovativeness (innovation adoption life cycle) in a population from the IDC perspective and the segments where the three case study companies are located. The figure shows that ADC Telehealth Ltd is still operating at the innovators' segment with its 0.1% adoption rate, while both GHI Ltd (with 3.55%) and DEF Ltd (with 4.67%) are at the early adopters' segment. Innovation, according to the authors, will spread (and businesses will become sustainable) when they evolve to meet the needs of successive segments (source: Oderanti and Li 2018)

Goodhue and Thompson (1995) developed the TTF model (see Fig. 2.6). Their research highlights the importance of the fit between users' tasks and technologies in achieving individual performance effects from information technology (Goodhue and Thompson 1995). From the point of view of this thesis, TTF is viewed as a tool to evaluate whether information systems and services are meeting users' needs. Simultaneously, TTF focuses on the match between user task needs and the available functionality of the IT (Dishaw and Strong 1999). TTF posits that IT will be used if, and only if, the functions available to users support (fit) their activities. Individual skills, operationalised as computer literacy, negatively affect between task and technology and, operationalised as experience with the specific new technology, positively affect usage (Dishaw and Strong 1999).

In other words, TTF is the degree to which a technology assists individuals in performing their portfolio of tasks and is the correspondence of task requirements, individual abilities and functionality of technologies.

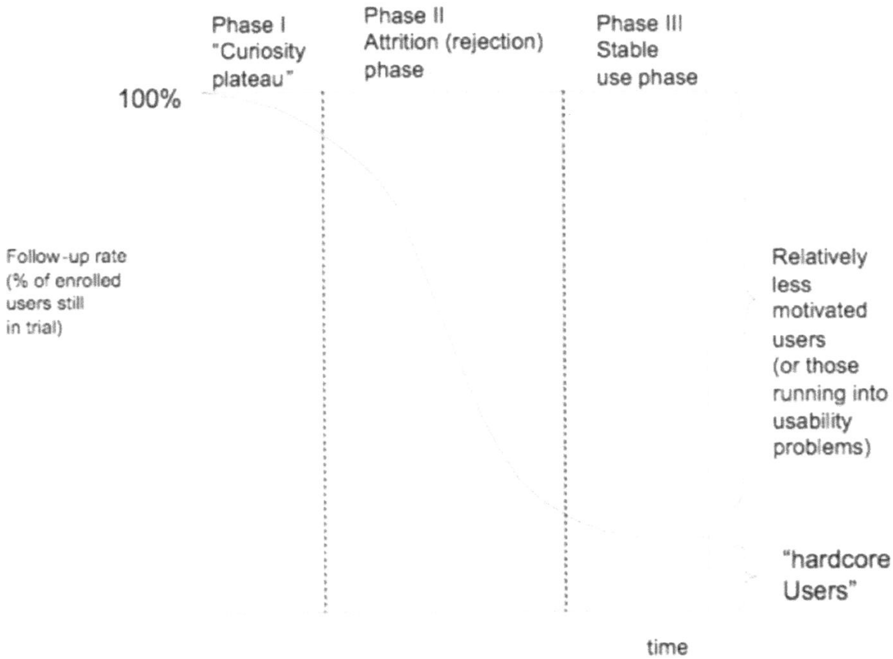

Fig. 2.5 The attrition curve. In Figure 2.5, the curve presents three phases. There is an initial phase where individuals use eHealth solutions out of curiosity. This phase is followed by the attrition (or rejection) stage where people realise the actual benefits of the solution. Lastly, phase three presents a 'stable user group—hardcore users'—who continue to utilise the solution (source: Eysenbach 2005)

Other significant bodies of research on human behaviours are the Motivational Model (MM) and the SCT. Within the business management field, Davis et al. (1992) applied the theory of motivation to understand and use new technology. The model distinguishes between extrinsic motivation, the concept that users will want to perform an activity because it is perceived to be instrumental in achieving valued outcomes that are distinct from the activity itself, such as improved job performance, pay or promotions and intrinsic motivation, the perception that users will want to perform an activity for no apparent reinforcement other than the process of performing the activity per se (Davis et al. 1992). As regards SCT, it is significant to report the core components: self-efficacy (ability to use a technology to accomplish a particular task), affect (an individual's liking for a particular behaviour), anxiety (evoking an emotional response when performing a behaviour) and outcome expectations (the performance-related or personal consequences of a behaviour; Compeau et al. 1999).

As the TTF, the TAM is specifically tailored for modelling users' acceptance of information systems or technologies. It is considered an adaptation of TRA to the study of IT utilisation (Ajzen and Fishbein 1980). It applies TRA in the sense that it focuses solely on the first component, that of expectations, and does not include the

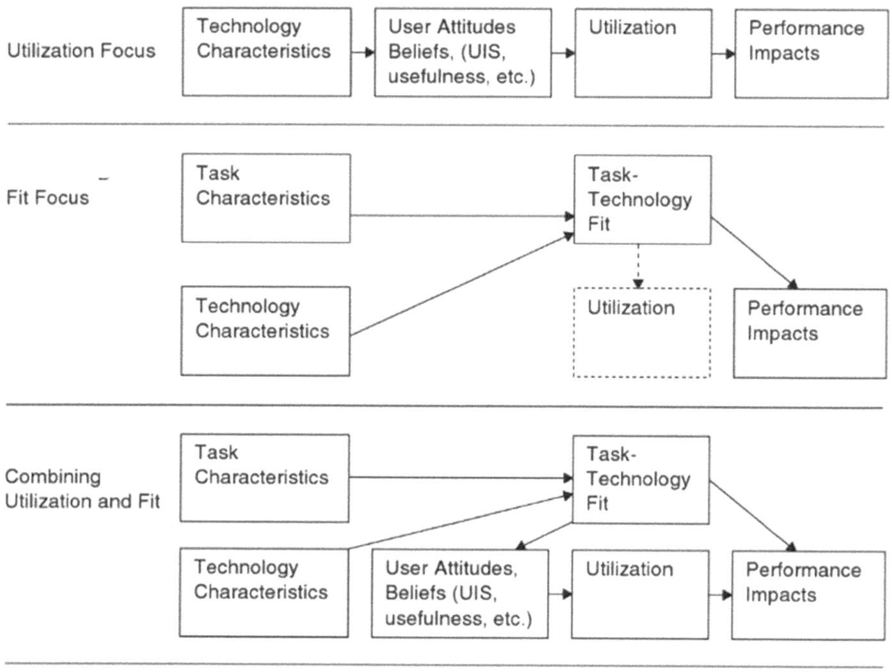

Fig. 2.6 Task–Technology Fit (TTF) model. Figure 2.6 shows the Task-Technology Fit theory, which holds that IT is more likely to have a positive impact on individual performance and be used if the capabilities of the IT match the tasks that the user must perform (source: Goodhue and Thompson 1995)

aspect of subjective standards, at least initially (Ogrezeanu 2015). Davis (1985) developed the TAM as a theoretical model with a narrow, dedicated focus on information technology adoption behaviour. In 1989, Davis et al. (1989) used this framework to explain the general determinants of computer acceptance. Since then, TAM has become an extremely widely used theoretical model in the study of technology adoption, and there are now numerous academic research papers citing the original article introducing TAM. A meta-analysis of TAM explains that during the past 18 years, the information system community has considered it a parsimonious and powerful theory.

The basic TAM model (see Fig. 2.7) includes and tests two specific beliefs: perceived usefulness (PU) and perceived ease (PE) of use (Davis 1989). PU is the degree to which individuals believe that using a particular system would enhance their job performance. There must be a positive user–performance relationship. PE refers to the degree to which an individual believes that using a particular system would be free of effort. The final version of TAM was developed by Davis and Venkatesh (1996). In the previous version, external variables that influence attitude towards use, intention of use and actual usage have effects on PE and PU. In Venkatesh and Davis version, PE and PU have a direct impact on behavioural intention. Lee et al. (2003) investigate the history of TAM by tracing major concepts.

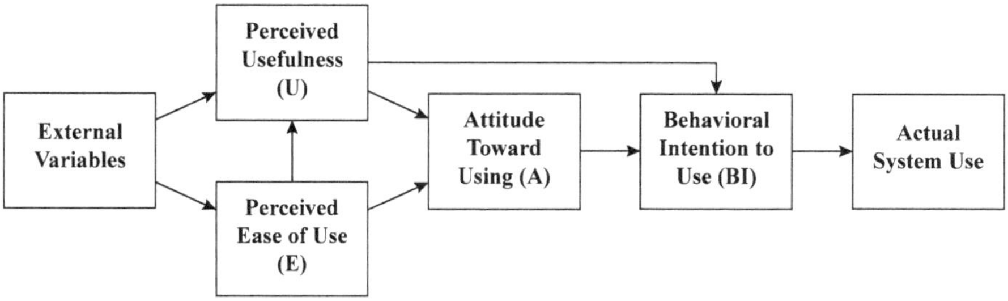

Fig. 2.7 Technology Acceptance Model (TAM). Figure 2.7 shows the Technology Acceptance Model (TAM), an information systems theory that models how users come to accept and use a technology. The actual system use is the desired end point where everyone will be able to use the technology, and hence, behavioural intention has to be formed, which is a factor that leads people to use the technology. The behavioural intention is influenced by the attitude, which is the general impression regarding the technology among individuals (source: Davis, F. D. (1989), Perceived usefulness, perceived ease of use, and user acceptance of information technology, MIS Quarterly, 13(3): 319–340)

They divide the history into four periods: introduction, validation, extension and elaboration. In the first period, TAM was a much simpler, easier to use and more powerful model of the determinant of user acceptance of computer technology than TRA. In the validation period, studies during this time investigated extensively whether TAM instruments were strong, stable, accurate and true and found these properties to be reliable. The third and the last period culminated in the introduction of TAM 2, after a period of studies on determinants.

Venkatesh and Davis (2000) suggested TAM 2. It theorises that the mental evaluation by users of the match between important goals at work and the results of conducting job tasks using the programme serves as a basis for generating expectations as regards the system's utility. In other words, TAM 2 (see Fig. 2.8) has been proposed to better understand the determinants of perceived utility of organisational interference and how it influences changes over time with that programme experience. Simultaneously, external factors are substituted for social influence processes (subjective norm, voluntariness and image) and cognitive instrumental processes (job relevance, output quality, result demonstrability and perceived ease of use). These factors significantly influence user acceptance.

Later, Venkatesh and Bala (2008) combined TAM 2 with the perceived user-friendly determinants model by Venkatesh and developed an integrated Technology Acceptance Model called TAM 3. They suggest investigating the influence of organisational intervention. The TAM 3 research model was tested in real-world settings of IT implementations (Venkatesh and Bala 2008). This study presents more detailed explanations on the reasons that users consider a given framework useful at three points in time: pre-implementation, 1-month post-implementation and 3 months post-implementation. Intervention in pre-implementation describes a series of organisational tasks during the programme development and deployment and can potentially lead to the greater acceptance of a system by minimising initial resistance and providing a realistic preview of the new system.

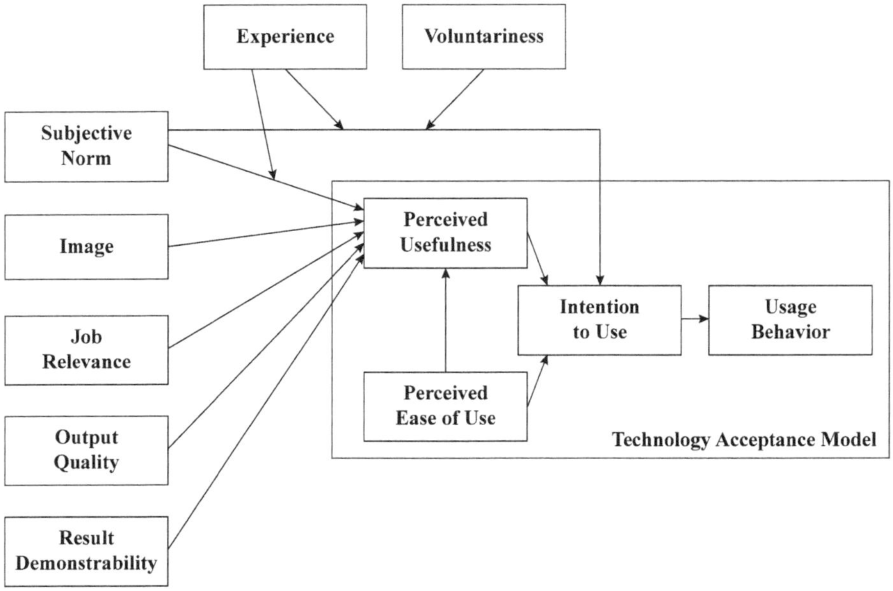

Fig. 2.8 Technology Acceptance Model (TAM 2). Figure 2.8 shows a graphic overview of the model, referred to as TAM 2. The TAM 2 model added, 'theoretical constructs involving social influence processes (subjective norm, voluntariness, and image) and cognitive instrumental processes (job relevance, output quality, result demonstrability, and perceived ease of use)'. (Source: Venkatesh and Davis 2000)

Pre-implementation intervention (also termed 'anchor') is presented in five categories: design characteristics, user participation, management support and management and incentive alignment (as in Fig. 2.9). Post-implementation intervention (also termed 'adjustment') is a collection of operational, administrative and support activities that occur after a programme is implemented to improve the system's user acceptance level. This intervention is important in helping the user go through the initial shock and changes associated with the new system.

The post-implementation intervention is presented in three categories: training, organisational support and peer support.

In 2003, Venkatesh et al. formulated the Unified Theory of Acceptance and Use of Technology (UTAUT), as shown in Fig. 2.10. They theorised that four components have a significant role in usage behaviour and user acceptance: performance expectancy, effort expectancy, social influence and facilitating conditions (Venkatesh et al. 2003). Thus, UTAUT can be considered a unified view of previous works. In particular, it is based on an integration of TRA, TAM, TBM, MM, IDT and SCT (Lai 2017), which have been discussed in this chapter.

Performance expectancy is defined as the degree to which individuals believe that using the system will help them to attain gains in job performance. The five

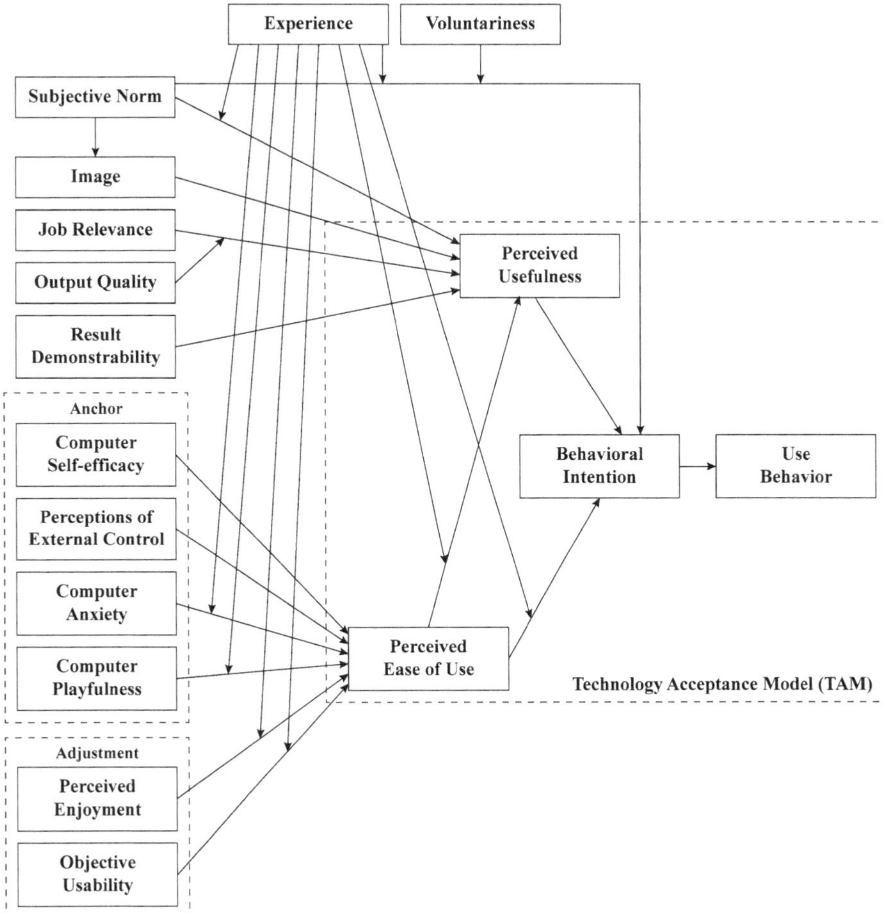

Fig. 2.9 Technology Acceptance Model (TAM 3). Figure 2.9 shows the Technology Acceptance Model 3 (TAM3) as an inclusive, complex model that emphasises the processes that relate to perceived usefulness and perceived ease of use. The model suggests that predictors for perceived usefulness will not influence the perceived ease of use and vice versa (source: Venkatesh and Bala 2008)

constructs that pertain to these components are extrinsic motivation in MM, relative advantage in IDT, outcome expectation in SCT and the perceived usefulness in TAM. At the same time, for UTAUT there is reason to expect that the relationship between performance expectancy and behavioural intention is mediated by gender and age. Gender and age will reduce the impact of performance expectations on behavioural intention, and hence, the effect will be greater for men and particularly for younger men.

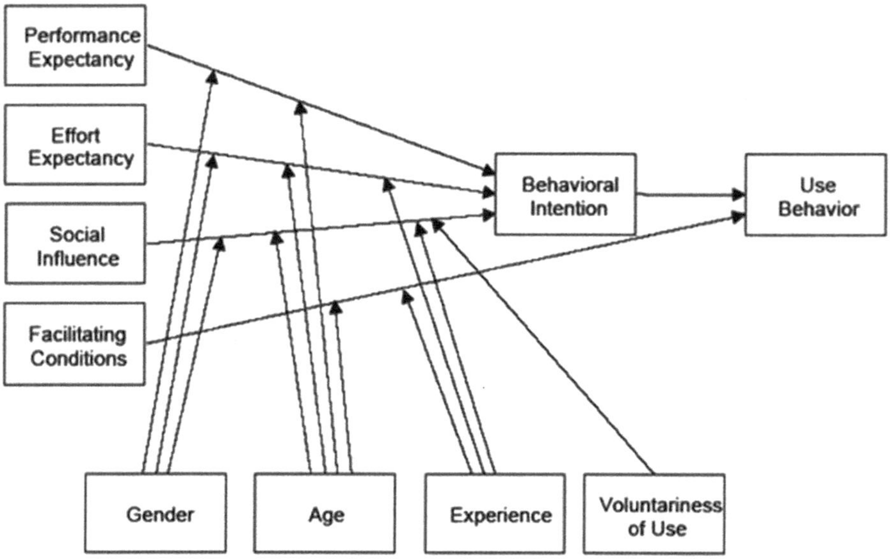

Fig. 2.10 Unified Theory of Acceptance and Use of Technology (UTAUT). Figure 2.10 shows UTAUT, which aims to explain user intentions to use an information system and subsequent usage behaviour. The theory holds that four key constructs (performance expectancy, effort expectancy, social influence and facilitating conditions) are direct determinants of usage intention and behaviour. Gender, age, experience and voluntariness of use are posited to moderate the impact of the four key constructs on usage intention and behaviour (source: Venkatesh, Morris, Davis and Davis 2003)

Effort expectancy is defined as the degree of ease associated with the use of the system. Perceived ease of use and complexity in TAM and use in IDT are clearly the constructs from the existing models. The hypothesis is that effort expectancy is mediated by gender, age and experience and, thus, the effect is greater for women, especially younger women, particularly in the early stages of the experience.

Social influence is defined as the degree to which an individual perceives that important others believe they should use the new system. The root constructs of these components are subjective norm in TRA/TAM and image in IDT. The role of social influence in decisions to embrace technology is complex and subject to a wide variety of contingent influences. Gender, age, voluntariness and experience may reduce the impact of social influence on behavioural purpose, such that the effect will be greater for women, especially older women, particularly in the early stages of experience in compulsory settings. Facilitating conditions are defined as the degree to which an individual believes that an organisational and technical infrastructure exists to support use of the system. This component embodies the perceived behavioural control of TBP and DTBP and compatibility of IDT. The impact of facilitating conditions on use will be moderated by age and experience, and therefore, the effect for older workers will be greater, particularly with increased experience.

2.3 Insight on the Use of UTAUT for eHealth

Several research works have used these models, mainly TAM and UTAUT, to examine technology acceptance within healthcare organisations. Many previous studies have adopted and expanded TAM and UTAUT with additional constructs. Nuq (2009) applies UTAUT to investigate eHealth marketing services in developing countries. Further, Seligman (2001) explores the attitude of physicians, nurses and health system executives towards acceptance of an electronic health record (EHR) application by using TAM. Chiu (2010) applies UTAUT in eHealth services among Chinese Canadians caring for a family member with dementia. Kowitlawakul (2008) uses TAM to examine the applicability of the model in explaining nurses' acceptance of Telemedicine technology in a healthcare setting. Aldosari (2004) also uses TAM to examine physician attitudes towards EHR adoption. Moreover, Sintonen (2008) examines the willingness of customers in Finland to adopt technologies in healthcare services by using TAM.

All these contributions confirm the hypothesis that some of these models are suitable for investigating the reasons for the adoption/non-adoption of innovative tools in the field of eHealth.

From the careful review of the literature proposed by Ami-Narh and Williams (2012), it is possible to clearly state that some studies have aimed at investigating the adoption of tools referable to eHealth (Chau and Hu 2001; Han et al. 2006; Hu et al. 1999; Liang et al. 2003; Schaper and Pervan 2007; Wang et al. 2009), but always from the perspective of economic/health policy, sociology or medicine.

The originality of the present research lies in instead aiming to investigate the choices of adoption/non-adoption of eHealth systems not so much of operators in the public health sector, as of operators of community-based health practices. In particular, the following chapter intends to refer to aspects that have been expressed in Chap. 1, namely, the propensity to use such systems and the factors determining the choices of adoption/non-adoption by private health professionals, such as pharmacists, who are now called in Italy to address the choice of adhering to the Telemedicine programmes proposed by the government, which are still not implemented locally. In the study of the factors that influence the choice of adoption or non-adoption, reference will be made to the UTAUT model for three specific reasons:

- UTAUT is one of the most innovative research models, which already carries the constructs of many previous models, as explained in the previous paragraph.
- UTAUT is relatively little used in eHealth research thus far, and its structure is believed to allow identification of the reasons that determine, or even predict, the reasons behind the choice to adopt Telemedicine.
- UTAUT, compared with the other research models, appears to be of more immediate use in the administration of a survey, and this is a prelude to higher redemption rates compared with other models, which, to remain simple, risk ending up being not entirely complete as regards the quality of the inferable information they provide.

In addition, the literature relating to the theories of technology adoption shows that UTAUT has the highest power in explaining behaviour intention and usage compared with all the other theories proposed thus far (Ami-Narh and Williams 2012; Venkatesh et al. 2003). UTAUT also provides better understanding about the factors that determine behaviour intentions (Venkatesh et al. 2003).

Therefore, the next chapter will provide as complete as possible a picture of the options for adopting Telemedicine tools for pharmacies in Italy. Telemedicine shows enormous potential in terms of greater access to care and efficiency, yet the acceptance of this modality of assistance (by health professionals and pharmacists in the first place) is still to be tested.

References

Ajzen I (1985) From intentions to actions: A theory of planned behavior. In J. Kuhl & J. Beckmann (Eds.), *Action control: From cognition to behavior*. Berlin, Heidelber, New York: Springer-Verlag. (pp. 11–39)

Ajzen H, Fishbein M (1980) Understanding attitudes and predicting social behavior. Englewood Cliffs, N.J.: Prentice-Hall

Aldosari BMB (2004) Factors affecting physicians' attitudes about the medical information system usage and acceptance through the mandated implementation of integrated medical information system at the Saudi Arabia National Guard Health System: A modified technology acceptance model. Dissertation. University of Pittsburgh

Ami-Narh JT, Williams PA (2012) A revised UTAUT model to investigate E-health acceptance of health professionals in Africa. J Emerg Trends Comput Inf Sci 3(10):1383–1391

Chau PY, Hu PJH (2001) Information technology acceptance by individual professionals: A model comparison approach. Decis Sci 32(4):699–719

Chiu ML (2010) Usage and non-usage behaviour of eHealth services among Chinese Canadians caring for a family member with dementia.. Dissertation

Compeau D, Higgins CA, Huff S (1999) Social cognitive theory and individual reactions to computing technology: A longitudinal study. MIS Q 23(2):145–158

Davis FD (1985) A technology acceptance model for empirically testing new end-user information systems: Theory and results. Thesis, Massachusetts Institute of Technology. https://dspace.mit.edu/handle/1721.1/15192. Accessed 10 December 2019

Davis FD (1989) Perceived usefulness, perceived ease of use, and user acceptance of information technology. MIS Q 13(3):319–340

Davis FD, Venkatesh V (1996) A critical assessment of potential measurement biases in the technology acceptance model: three experiments. Int J Hum Comp Stud 45(1):19–45

Davis FD, Bagozzi RP, Warshaw PR (1989) User acceptance of computer technology: a comparison of two theoretical models. Manag Sci 35(8):982–1003

Davis FD, Bagozzi RP, Warshaw PR (1992) Extrinsic and intrinsic motivation to use computers in the workplace. J Appl Soc Psychol 22(14):1111–1132

Dishaw MT, Strong DM (1999) Extending the technology acceptance model with task–technology fit constructs. Inf Manag 36(1):9–21

Eysenbach G (2005) The law of attrition. J Med Internet Res 7(1):e11

van Gemert-Pijnen JE, Nijland N, van Limburg M et al (2011) A holistic framework to improve the uptake and impact of eHealth technologies. J Med Internet Res 13(4):e111

Goodhue DL, Thompson RL (1995) Task-technology fit and individual performance. MIS Q 19(2):213–236

Han S, Mustonen P, Seppanen M, Kallio M (2006) Physicians' acceptance of mobile communication technology: an exploratory study. Int J Mob Commun 4(2):210–230
Hu PJ, Chau PY, Sheng ORL, Tam KY (1999) Examining the technology acceptance model using physician acceptance of telemedicine technology. J Manag Inf Syst 16(2):91–112
Kowitlawakul Y (2008) Technology acceptance model: predicting nurses' acceptance of telemedicine technology (eICU). George Mason University, Virginia (USA)
Lai PC (2017) The literature review of technology adoption models and theories for the novelty technology. J Inf Syst Tech Manag 14(1):21–38
Lee Y, Kozar KA, Larsen KRT (2003) The technology acceptance model: past, present, and future. Comm AIS 12:50
Liang H, Xue Y, Byrd TA (2003) PDA usage in healthcare professionals: testing an extended technology acceptance model. Int J Mob Commun 1(4):372–389
Nuq PA (2009) Innovation adoption (behavioral intention) for eHealth services in developing countries: a conceptual framework. J Int Univ Geneva Bus Rev 2(1):75–80
Oderanti FO, Li F (2018) Commercialization of eHealth innovations in the market of the UK healthcare sector: a framework for a sustainable business model. Psychol Mark 35(2):120–137
Ogrezeanu A (2015) Models of technology adoption: an integrative approach. Netw Intell Stud 3(05):55–67
Rogers EM (2010) Diffusion of innovations, 4th edn. Simon & Schuster, New York
Schaper LK, Pervan GP (2007) ICT and OTs: A model of information and communication technology acceptance and utilisation by occupational therapists. Int J Med Inform 76:S212–S221
Scherer M, Craddock G (2002) Matching Person & Technology (MPT) assessment process. Tech Disabil 14:125–131
Seligman LS (2001) Perceived value impact as an antecedent of perceived usefulness, perceived ease of use, and attitude: a perspective on the influence of values on technology acceptance.. Dissertation.
Sintonen S (2008) Older consumers adopting information and communication technology: evaluating opportunities for health care applications. Lappeenranta University Technology, Finland
Venkatesh V, Bala H (2008) Technology Acceptance Model 3 and a research agenda on interventions. Decis Sci 39(2):273–315
Venkatesh V, Davis FD (2000) A theoretical extension of the technology acceptance model: four longitudinal field studies. Manag Sci 46(2):186–204
Venkatesh V, Morris MG, Davis GB, Davis FD (2003) User acceptance of information technology: toward a unified view. MIS Q 27(3):425–478
Wang CJ, Patel MH, Schueth AJ et al (2009) Perceptions of standards-based electronic prescribing systems as implemented in outpatient primary care: a physician survey. J Am Med Inform Assoc 16(4):493–502

Chapter 3
Telemedicine as an eHealth Tool for Empowering Community-Based Private Health Professionals in the Italian Context

Abstract eHealth, an evolving field in medical informatics and public health, involves delivering health services using information and communication technology (ICT) tools. Its introduction has improved healthcare delivery quality across health sectors and hospitals. The term eHealth is frequently used in academia and professional bodies in the healthcare domain. eHealth includes delivering health information and education over the Internet along with commercial products used by health professionals and patients to make healthcare delivery more efficient. It comprises a wide variety of clinical activities delivered through the Internet. Telemedicine, especially using two-way interactive audio/video communications and computers to deliver health services to remote patients, is an eHealth component. Both eHealth and Telemedicine are extensively used for facilitating remote monitoring and diagnosis, creating educational and health awareness and providing health education across geographical boundaries. In this chapter, we will focus on Telemedicine, as a possible eHealth tool. More precisely, we will briefly describe the European context, and subsequently, we will focus on the Italian context, where Telemedicine still appears to be an instrument difficult to understand and diffuse. Finally, we will focus on the need for training and information on Telemedicine and then provide a cost–benefit analysis regarding Telemedicine implementation.

Keywords Telemedicine · Decentralisation · Empowerment · Cost-effective ratio

3.1 eHealth and Telemedicine

As shown in Chap. 1 and Chap. 2, eHealth is an evolving field in medical informatics and public health in which health services are delivered using information and communication technology (ICT) tools. The introduction of eHealth has improved the quality of healthcare delivery across health sectors and hospitals (Litvak and Fineberg 2013). The term eHealth is frequently used in academic institutions and professional bodies in the healthcare domain. eHealth includes health information

N. Cobelli, *Innovation in Community-Based Private Practices Through eHealth*, International Series in Advanced Management Studies,
https://doi.org/10.1007/978-3-030-48177-3_3

and educational delivery over the Internet along with commercial products that are used by health professionals and patients to make healthcare delivery more efficient. Thus, eHealth comprises a wide variety of clinical activities that are delivered through the Internet. Telemedicine, which also uses ICT, especially two-way interactive audio/video communications and computers to deliver health services to remote patients, is a component of eHealth. Both eHealth and Telemedicine are extensively used for facilitating remote monitoring and diagnosis, creating educational and health awareness and providing health education across geographical boundaries.

Telemedicine is a method of providing healthcare services through the use of innovative technologies, in particular, ICTs, in situations in which the health professional and the patient (or two health professionals) are not in the same geographical location. It involves the secure transmission of medical data and health information in the form of texts, sounds, images or other forms necessary for the prevention and diagnosis of disease and for the treatment and subsequent monitoring of patients. Telemedicine services must be integrated into any diagnostic/therapeutic healthcare services. However, this service cannot replace the traditional health service in the doctor–patient personal relationship—rather, both services are combined to potentially improve treatment efficacy and appropriateness. Telemedicine must also comply with all the legal obligations of the applicable health act. Of note, the use of ICT tools to share information on health treatments and to share medical data and/or health information online does not constitute provision of Telemedicine services. As an example, Telemedicine does not include health-related services involving information portals, social networks, forums, newsgroups and e-mails.

Telemedicine can be used for the following health purposes:

- Secondary prevention: These are services dedicated to people already classified at risk or already with pathologies (e.g. diabetes or cardiovascular pathologies), who, although leading a normal life, must undergo constant monitoring of some vital parameters, such as the blood sugar level for those with diabetes, to reduce the risk of the onset of complications.
- Diagnosis: These are services that aim to move patients' diagnostic information instead of them. A complete diagnostic procedure is difficult to perform through the use of Telemedicine tools alone, but Telemedicine can complement, or allow useful insights into, the diagnosis and treatment process, for example, by making it possible to use diagnostic tests reported by the specialist, at the general practitioner's surgery, the pharmacy or the patient's home (Federfarma 2019).
- Care: These are services aimed at making therapeutic choices and assessing the prognostic trend regarding patients for whom a clear diagnosis is available. Examples include teledialysis services and remote surgery.
- Rehabilitation: These are services provided at home, or other care facilities provided to individuals who are prescribed rehabilitation, since they are fragile, children, elderly or with a disability or a chronic disease (Chen et al. 2017) or are patients (Newman et al. 2004). It is the management, also over time, of vital

parameters, defining the exchange of data (on vital parameters) between the patient (at home, in the pharmacy or in a dedicated care facility) in connection with a monitoring station for data interpretation.

Telemedicine services can be classified into the following macro categories:

- Specialised Telemedicine
- Teleassistance

3.1.1 Specialised Telemedicine

The Specialised Telemedicine category includes the various ways in which remote medical services are provided within a specific medical discipline. It can occur between doctor and patient or between doctors and other healthcare professionals. Depending on the type of relationship between the actors involved, Specialised Telemedicine (D'Andreamatteo et al. 2015) can be performed in the following ways:

- Televisit is a sanitary act in which the doctor interacts remotely with the patient. The consequent medical act of diagnosis can result in the prescription of drugs or treatments. During a Televisit, a health worker in the patient's area can assist the doctor. The connection must allow the doctor to see and interact with the patient and must take place in real or deferred time.
- Teleconsultation is used in deciding on a diagnosis and/or a choice of therapy without the physical presence of the patient. This is a remote consultancy activity between doctors that allows a doctor to seek the advice of one or more doctors, who have the specific training and competence required, on the basis of medical information related to patient care.
- Health remote control is an act consisting of the assistance provided by a doctor or other health worker to another doctor or health worker engaged in a health act. The term is also used for the advice provided to those who provide emergency assistance.
- Local Telemedicine services provided by General Practitioners (GPs) and Free Choice Paediatricians (PLS) can be included in Specialised Telemedicine.

3.1.2 Teleassistance

Teleassistance means a social assistance system for taking care of the elderly or a frail person at home (see Censis 2017), by managing alarms and activating emergency services and 'support' calls from a service centre. Teleassistance has a mainly social content, with blurred boundaries towards the health content, with which it should connect to guarantee continuity of care.

3.2 Telemedicine: New Opportunities, Challenges and Needs for Italian Community-Based Private Practices

The ongoing evolution of the demographic dynamics and the consequent modification of the health needs of the population, with an increasing share of the elderly and of those with chronic diseases, make it essential to redesign the structure and organisation of the service network, especially with a view to strengthening the area territorial assistance (Kaplan et al. 2015; Propper et al. 2008, 2010). Technological innovation can contribute to a reorganisation of healthcare, in particular, by supporting a focus shift in healthcare from the hospital to the territory, through innovative citizen-centred assistance models and by facilitating access to services in the national territory. This support is critical because the provision of health and socio-health services enabled by Telemedicine is fundamental in this sense, helping to ensure equity in the access to care in remote territories, support for the management of chronic conditions, a channel of access to high specialisation, better continuity of care through multidisciplinary discussion and a fundamental aid for emergency–urgency services.

Many Telemedicine initiatives have been launched at the national level, which too often, however, refer to experiments, prototypes and projects characterised by limited cases and high mortality of the initiative. Given this inorganic diffusion of health services provided using Telemedicine methods, developing a shared governance model of these initiatives, which must have as the central point specific knowledge about the health sector, is essential. Therefore, it is necessary to harmonise the guidelines and application models of Telemedicine as a prerequisite to ensure the interoperability of Telemedicine services and to transition from an experimental logic to a structured logic of the use of these services. In this context, in 2010, the Minister of Health pro tempore Prof Ferruccio Fazio established a working table for Telemedicine, in the Superior Health Council (CSS) in Italian, consisting of members of the CSS, Ministry officials and CSS experts. Taking into account the priorities of the National Health System (NHS) and in line with the initiatives undertaken at the community level, the table has set itself the objective of creating enabling conditions for diffusing Telemedicine services concretely integrated into clinical practice, with which to provide effective responses to the modified needs of health of citizens.

3.2.1 *The European Context*

The relevance of Telemedicine and its impact on society and health are recognised internationally. The Communication of the European Commission COM (2008) 689 on 'Telemedicine for the benefit of patients, health systems and society', issued by the European Commission on 4 November 2008, is aimed at supporting member states in the implementation, on a large scale, of Telemedicine services through specific initiatives, such as creating trust in Telemedicine services, favouring their acceptance, bringing legal clarity, solving technical problems and facilitating market development. As part of the aforementioned communication, the European Commission has identified specific actions to be taken at the member-state level. In particular, these actions require each member state to assess its Telemedicine needs and priorities, so that they become an integral part of the national health strategies, and to assess and adapt their respective national regulations to allow broader access to Telemedicine services, addressing issues such as accreditation, liability, reimbursements and protection of privacy and personal data. The European Economic and Social Committee, on 23 December 2009, expressed an opinion on COM Communication (2008) 689. In the conclusion of this document, Telemedicine is defined as a type of 'cultural revolution', the development of which must be seen in the context of a general evolution of health policies and systems. The document also underlines the need for users of the healthcare system (e.g. patient organisations and healthcare professionals) to be involved at the national level in defining the methods of development and financing of the new Telemedicine technologies.

In addition, in the Digital Agenda prepared by the European Commission for the implementation of the Europe 2020 plan, which was made official on 19 August 2010, a specific 'key action' is envisaged on which the European Commission intends to focus along with the interested member states and stakeholders, with the aim of spreading Telemedicine services (by December 2020). In many European countries, Telemedicine is widely used, and in some cases, it is supported by regulatory interventions, strategic documents and national-level projects. Next, we describe some salient aspects of the strategies that some countries have adopted regarding eHealth and, more specifically, Telemedicine, in a representative, non-exhaustive way. In Sweden, the National Strategy for eHealth was published in 2006. It is an evolving document, developed through a series of regular reports (the latest version in 2010). Telemedicine in Sweden is widespread: in 2008, it was in use in more than 100 applications and 75% of hospitals. The main application areas are Televisit (patient–doctor visits), Telemonitoring and radiological Teleconsultation. Norway has also invested in eHealth solutions because Telemedicine is relevant owing to the low population density and the large distances people must travel to reach the nearest hospital. It has many applications in use, including Teleconsultation between GPs and specialists, telepathology, teleradiology, telepsychiatry and services for improving cancer treatment.

In Spain, the Regional Health Systems, which are part of the NHS, have focused attention on eHealth in the past 15 years and have adopted some common lines of action, including the development of Telemedicine systems or services. In Great Britain, the Department of Health funded a vast Teleservice and Telesalute programme in May 2008, the Whole System Demonstrator Programme, aimed at fragile people and those with a chronic illness, which involved over 6000 patients and over 200 doctors in 2 years, probably the largest systematic experimentation in Telemedicine ever conducted. The study results are such as to encourage the Department of Health towards a new programme (the 'Three Million Lives' campaign) in collaboration with industry, the NHS, professional associations and social organisations, aimed at a potential three million candidates who could benefit from Teleassistance and Telehealth services. As regards France, the Ministry of Health published Decree 20101–1229 of 19 October 2010 in the journal *Officiel de la République Francaise*, which defines Telemedicine services, determines the conditions of implementation and assesses the organisational aspects for recognising Telemedicine within the NHS.

3.2.2 The Italian Context

Telemedicine experiences at the national, regional and local levels are manifold (Centro Nazionale per la Telemedicina e le Nuove Tecnologie Assistenziali 2018). To evaluate and monitor the applications of Telemedicine, following a special agreement stipulated with the Ministry of Health, the Emilia Romagna Region, with the participation of the regions of Tuscany, Liguria, Marche and Campania, to which have been added the regions of Veneto, Sicily and Lombardy, established the National e-Care Observatory in 2007. The Observatory aims to build a map of e-care networks to encourage the exchange of good practices and related technologies, for improving the accessibility and effectiveness of the services provided online to citizens (Ministero della Salute, Mappatura Nazionale. http://www.salute.gov.it. Accessed 15 Jan 2020). The establishment of the Observatory also takes into account the European strategies to achieve the eHealth objectives of the national health plan, with particular reference to the management of patients with a chronic disease, fragile patients and continuity of care. This Observatory, initially focused on home care, is gradually extending its perimeter to all areas of Telemedicine to define a reference model at the national level. To have a clear and complete vision of the Telemedicine project initiatives activated in the national territory, a tool has been made available within the Observatory to the regions, which allows the online compilation of forms relating to the projects in the regional territory. Therefore, in the fact sheets, the description of the projects, the type of services and related areas of application, the progress of the projects and the type of recipient of the service, as well as the territorial scope of the project, have been reported. Moreover, the Armed Forces have supported for years the development of military Telemedicine aimed at military operations and also at humanitarian missions as an instrument of peace-making action. Italian Civil Protection Agency has developed models of Telemedicine as part of its activities in emergencies and in interventions in disasters. Finally, the CIRM (International Radio-Medical Centre), founded in 1935, fulfils the role of the national Telemedicine Assistance Service in the field of search and rescue systems, both on the sea and for air navigation.

As presented in Chap. 1, the face of the pharmacy has changed following the three ministerial decrees of 16 December 2010 and 8 July on the 'service pharmacy', which provided for the provision of services and professional services to citizens paid for by families. As early as 18 November 2010, Minister Fazio had received a favourable opinion from the Italian 'Permanent Conference for Relations between the State, the Regions and the Italian Autonomous Provinces' regarding the possibility of introducing new services that can be provided by local pharmacies, which are in all respects community-based private practices. The three decrees are as follows:

- Discipline of the limits and conditions of the first instance analytical services, falling within the scope of self-control and for the technical indications relating to the instrumental devices (Decree of 16 December 2010)
- Delivery of specific professional services by pharmacies (Decree of 16 December 2010)
- Provision by pharmacies of booking outpatient specialist care services, payment of the relative share of the citizen's expense and collection of reports relating to outpatient specialist care services (Decree of 8 July 2011)

In this work, we are particularly interested in Telemedicine, contained in the first of the listed decrees.

Overall, the decree aims to reduce the waiting times for health services (as documented by Mariotti et al. 2014). Indeed, all states have the problem of long waiting times (Mariotti et al. 2008), where there is a universal health system that offers a minimum level of assistance to the citizen (Nuti and Vainieri 2012).

The Italian Ministry of Health itself describes this phenomenon as one of the most critical points of modern health systems (Regione Lombardia 2017), given that it compromises the accessibility and usability of the services to be provided. Hence, the reduction of waiting times (Rebba 2009; Rebba and Rizzi 2011; Viberg et al. 2013) is a primary objective of the NHS, and the provision of services, within appropriate times with respect to the pathology and need for treatment, represents a structural component of the essential levels of assistance, as defined by the Italian Decree of the President of the Council of Ministers (DPCM) of 29 November 2001 and by the DPCM of 12 January 2017.

A waiting list for the delivery of health services is generated in case of a misalignment between the demand (the request for health services by citizens) and the offer (number of examinations and visits that the health system is able to provide; Mohammadshahi et al. 2019; Rose et al. 2011; Van der Voort et al. 2010, 2014).

The phenomenon is partly related to the scarcity of funds to be allocated owing to the increase in the offer (De Belvis et al. 2013) but also, and above all, to a non-rational use of the available resources (planning and programming of the offer) and to the application of a management model of the service delivery cycle (prescription, booking and delivery) that is not always optimal (Mehrotra et al. 2008; Moraros et al. 2016; Murray and Berwick 2003; Murray and Tantau 2000).

Patients who benefit from outpatient specialist services are the users of health services for whom health conditions and the necessary diagnostic and therapeutic treatments do not require hospitalisation of several days but access that lasts, at the maximum, throughout the day (LaGanga 2011). Therefore, the definition of outpatient specialist care includes various diagnostic and therapeutic clinical care measures and, in particular:

- Specialist outpatient visits
- Laboratory services
- Diagnostic imaging services
- Rehabilitation and therapeutic services

The path of the citizen who needs an outpatient service can be simplified to five fundamental consecutive steps (Ballini et al. 2015):

- t0: The citizen identifies a health problem and turns to a doctor.
- t1: The doctor prescribes an outpatient service.
- t2: The patient obtains the reservation for the service.
- t3: The actual supply of the service occurs.
- t4: The specialist prepares the report.

The interval between t2 (booking) and t3 (delivery) is generally considered 'waiting time', which represents the most significant component of the route and is perceived by the citizen as such. However, even the interval between t1 (prescription) and t2 (reservation), defined as 'contact time', can depend on severe system problems (e.g. long times in many locations that force the citizen to perform a long search and poor information on the dispensers and access methods), as well as the discretionary behaviour of the individual patient (e.g. underestimation of the problem, personal commitments and difficulty in moving).

Supply and demand in healthcare are not automatically aligned, as is usually the case in other areas of the economy, particularly in the field of economics and service management. The supply of health services is always 'chasing' the demand, which tends to increase and not to be 'reached'.

Many factors determine a continuous increase in health demand. In particular:

- Continuous innovations in the health sector (technology updates and development of new treatments)
- The progressive ageing of the population, associated with an ever-increasing prevalence of chronic diseases with complex care needs
- The increase in the population's awareness of the state of health as well as the emergence of new health needs as scientific knowledge increases
- The segmentation of the current health service, based on a 'provider-centred' model and segmented among several 'super-specialisations', which, for patients with complex care needs, implies the need to book multiple appointments, often on different dates and at different places

Although closely related to each other and often used interchangeably, 'waiting lists' and 'waiting times' indicate very different concepts (Fournier et al. 2012; Siciliani 2005). The term waiting list indicates a list that expresses the number of applications registered for a health service in relation to the time of satisfaction of the application itself (i.e. the number of patients who, at a given moment, still have to receive the service).

Conversely, the waiting time refers to the time necessary to satisfy the user's request on the list (i.e. the time elapsed between booking and provision of the service) and provides a measure of the accessibility of the service by citizens (Siciliani 2005, 2008, 2012; Siciliani et al. 2013, 2014). Therefore, individual patients are not interested in the length of the waiting list itself but in how long they will have to wait to receive a certain service (Siciliani et al. 2014).

The definition 'waiting time' includes two different moments of the patient's journey from booking to the actual delivery of the booking: access time and process time (or indirect and direct waiting time: Gupta and Denton 2008):

- The access time represents the time elapsed between the user's request for the service and the date set for the supply (order of magnitude: days).
- The process time is the difference between the time indicated to the patient for the appointment (or the patient's actual arrival in the clinic, if late) and the time when it is served by the specialist (order of magnitude: minutes).

If the process time is perceived more as an inconvenience for the patient, excessively long access times can be a serious public health problem. The process times have a significant impact on the efficiency of service delivery and therefore on the possibility of disposal of the waiting list, with positive repercussions also on access times (Siciliani 2012).

The waiting time for specialist outpatient services is an important indicator of access to treatment (Gutacker et al. 2016). It is, in fact, the phase preceding the meeting with the specialist or the execution of a diagnostic in-depth test, that moment when the disease is not yet fully characterised, in which, potentially, the greatest health risks occur related to waiting (Siciliani 2008).

In a healthcare system that provides only the implicit rationing of the demand represented by waiting times and manages the waiting list according to a 'first-come-first-served' access model, the wait for the public health service can determine for the user both the opportunity cost of time and a potential reduction in the health benefit obtainable from the performance of the service itself (Siciliani et al. 2014).

The opportunity cost of time, which is not always directly related to the level of economic capacity, includes costs related to the forced interruption of work (loss of income), study or leisure activities; the costs related to the time required to use the service (e.g. travel and process time); and 'anxiety' costs related to both the prolongation of the wait and the uncertainty of the exact moment in which it will be possible to access the service, which generate frustration and dissatisfaction with the system (Sampson et al. 2008).

During the waiting time, the patient's condition may worsen, improve spontaneously or remain unchanged until the performance is provided. For minor pathologies, the course of which proves to be positive even in the absence of medical intervention, after a certain time the performance may no longer be necessary or it could lead to limited benefits, without, however, causing a deterioration in the patient's health. Regardless, in some cases, waiting for a service that extends beyond a certain time threshold can lead to a reduction in the health benefit (e.g. greater duration of pain or disability and greater risk of a permanent reduction in the state of health). This is the case of diagnostic services which, in the face of particular patient symptoms, are necessary to ascertain the presence or absence of serious pathologies (e.g. neoplasms and cardiovascular diseases) or the therapies that the patient must undergo promptly after the ascertainment of a pathology with a certain level of severity. In reality, this criticality is mitigated in the current healthcare systems, in which the seriousness of the clinical picture directs the attribution to a specific class of priority for the delivery of the service in a suitable period.

In relation to these two aspects, a recent study by Landi et al. (2018) based on ISTAT surveys of 2013 demonstrates a disparity in access to care in the Italian population according to a socio-economic gradient. In particular, it was found that people with lower education and economic resources have a higher risk of facing longer waiting times for specialist visits, diagnostic tests and surgical operations, all of which are elements associated with the lower probability of early intervention and a higher mortality risk. This socio-economic gradient can be traced back to the so-called advocacy power: in particular, individuals from a low socio-economic level may have difficulty explaining their health condition correctly to the doctor for the recognition of the right priority, in interfacing with the system in remotely and informedly, in being fully aware of their rights and in exerting pressure in case of unjustified delays; in addition, they could reside in an area less provided with easily accessible health services. Therefore, the waiting time is configured as a 'non-monetary price' that risks undermining equity in access to care, which is the cardinal principle of the Italian NHS. In such a scenario, Telemedicine can be an affordable solution, based on two essential principles already presented in Chap. 1:

- Decentralisation of healthcare delivery
- Empowerment of community-based private practices

Of course, first, these two principles need the activities of information and training.

3.3 Information and Training on Telemedicine

To develop Telemedicine on a large scale, it is necessary to create trust in Telemedicine services and encourage their acceptance by healthcare professionals and patients. In this context, informing the patient regarding the use of Telemedicine and its likely benefits and training healthcare professionals and patients in using new technologies are fundamental aspects. In fact, since it is a technological innovation, it is essential that health professionals and patients are properly trained and prepared, and aware of their role and of the effectiveness of the service, to benefit patients and to ensure system efficiency.

Therefore, information and training actions are important to ensure the necessary professionalism and knowledge of the tools, as well as effective understanding of the interactive context in which they are used. In addition, Telemedicine can be very useful for providing specialist training content to operators and for assisting medical personnel in exercising their functions, especially in remote areas.

3.3.1 Information to Patients and Healthcare Professionals

The health act for which Telemedicine is used must not only comply with the rights and obligations inherent in any health act but also take into account the obligations related to its specificity, including providing information to the patient. The patient must be informed about the opportunity for, and scope of, the act, as well as about the means used and the methods for storing and processing data, in compliance with current legislation.

The wider diffusion of Telemedicine services, and in particular, Telemonitoring, raises new ethical concerns, especially as regards the changing relationships between patients and doctors. Therefore, it is essential that to accept these innovative service methods, the relationship between providers and recipients of healthcare must be defined to take into account the requirements of patients in need of human warmth and understandable, correct and reassuring information. In the relationship between healthcare professional and patient, it is important to ensure that the questions formulated, and the answers given, by the professional are understandable by the patient.

To respond to the fear of users and strengthen their trust, it is necessary to offer information programmes that allow patients to familiarise themselves with these new methods and tools, especially since they are often elderly people. Such information programmes could develop with the support of the European Commission and the involvement of representative organisations of patients, consumers and healthcare professionals, as well as voluntary organisations.

Concerning doctors and other health professionals (doctors in particular), many of them still suspect that Telemedicine may hinder or affect the relationship with their patients. Hence, it is necessary to provide doctors with more information on Telemedicine, interpreted as a simplification and improvement of the healthcare system procedures, especially those aimed at monitoring chronic diseases and making the patient's life easier, without detracting from the medical act or the patient's medical relationship.

3.3.2 Training and Empowerment of Patients

Despite the efforts to develop devices that are increasingly simple to use, patients assisted through Telemedicine systems require training, given that, for the most part, they are elderly patients, with little familiarity with technologies. However, the training of patients and caregivers must not be limited to technological aspects, but also be extended to the social and relationship aspects, on the change of the doctor–patient relationship and on the reassurance that, even at a distance, assistance and care are still guaranteed to the patient and pathology.

Further, the education and empowerment of the patient and caregivers must not be overlooked, particularly in the management of chronic diseases. The overall strategy for such management must move from a system that reacts to a sudden, unplanned event to a system that educates and empowers the patient to actively attend to the disease and comply with the treatment regimen. Preventing chronicity and improving the management of chronic pathology with the direct participation of the responsible patient represent a challenge for the economic sustainability of health systems.

3.3.3 Training and Updating of Health Professionals and New Professional Profiles

For the widespread dissemination of Telemedicine, particular attention must be paid to the training and updating of health professionals, to familiarise them with new methods for exercising their profession.

The training must focus on new information acquisition and equipment and data transmission technologies, which are the basis of a Telemedicine service. In addition, the continuity and coordination of healthcare also require the ability to use new tools for dialogue with the patient. Medical staff, especially those in contact with patients on the telephone or through the screen, must also have received psychological training to humanise the relationship at a distance and to remedy the lack of the physical presence on which the dialogue between doctor and patient had hitherto been based.

It is crucial that learning becomes a system action and not an extemporaneous proposal. Indeed, it is essential to implement a structured university training programme, combined with service training, aimed at optimising the use of Telemedicine to improve the quality of assistance. Specific university-level training will be gradually included in the training curricula of the health professions, in the first and second levels, as well as in post-graduate training. In addition, specific post-graduate training courses for eHealth, including Telemedicine, may be issued, which will provide university-level qualifications useful for professional employment at Dispensing Centres and Service Centres. Telemedicine should also be included among the topics covered by the Continuing Medical Education (ECM in Italian) and, in particular, in the context of the objective relating to technological innovation.

In a Telemedicine Centre, a fundamental role is played by professionals in technological fields, such as engineering and information technology. Moreover, the personnel assigned to the organisational management of the services may have an equally important role, depending on the complexity of the service. Thus, training programmes should also be aimed at these professionals who are directly involved in the implementation of a Telemedicine service.

3.4 Economic Evaluation of Telemedicine Services

We now introduce general criteria for the economic evaluation of Telemedicine programmes, which to date have not been widely shared and systematised. Among the most common economic evaluation methods, the following are recognised:

- Cost-Effectiveness Analysis (ACE): It considers both the costs and the results/outcomes of the programme and, specifically, compares the programme costs with its non-monetary results, such as 'years of life gained' and 'diseases avoided'.
- Cost–Benefit Analysis (ACB): It compares costs with benefits measured in monetary terms and presents the evaluation as a single unit of measurement (euro) but requires a conversion of results into economic value, with the identification of the factors of conversion.
- Cost–Utility Analysis (ACU): It measures the benefits in terms of utility (e.g. years of life gained weighted for quality and quality-adjusted life-years: QALYs).

Preliminary to economic evaluations is an analysis of costs, which identifies the resources used to provide the services of a specific programme. The costs to be considered are direct healthcare costs (e.g. hospital stay and laboratory tests) and non-healthcare costs (e.g. transport and assistance), as well as lost productivity costs (e.g. impact on family members and loved ones could also be assessed). Hence, from among these economic evaluation methods, we propose to adopt the ACE method since we consider it the one most applicable currently for the ex post evaluation of the results/outcomes of the Telemedicine services.

The implementation of ACE is aimed at comparing the costs and results of a given health programme, based on physical units of measurement, with those of alternative programmes for the same population. As a first approximation, the most obvious comparator should be represented by the current clinical practice. However, an opportunity is available to also consider a further hypothesis of intervention, depending on the scope of application of a specific Telemedicine programme, which is probably less expensive and with consolidated effectiveness in the territorial area of reference of the analysis. If actually existing, the latter benchmark hypothesis, which is further than current clinical practice, should be agreed upon and generalised to allow for a homogeneous comparison. The measurement of efficacy (i.e. objectively measurable improvements in the state of health attributable to the programme) presupposes the evaluation of final outcomes (e.g. the years of life gained) and intermediate outcomes (e.g. the avoided days of illness or the avoidance of criticality). The most immediate sources from which to draw on the data relating to efficacy are, mainly, scientific studies in the literature.

However, conducting experimental observation studies (pilot projects that allow cohort studies with follow-up and counterfactuals) could be particularly useful. These studies would enable us to obtain adequate transferability, and, even in consideration of the appropriate confidence intervals, it would be advisable to consider patients similar to the general population of patients who are potentially recipients of the Telemedicine service. However, determining the construction and size of the sample as well as the conduct of the entire study cannot be performed immediately and requires a prior definition of the specific objective of the Telemedicine project to be considered.

The measured elements, such as clinical efficacy indices, especially in relation to the final outcomes that can be measured in a suitably defined period, should be assigned a weight so that it is possible to determine a univocal value relating to the quality achieved, a comparable value, as a general logic, to the QALY indicator present in the ACU. Additional indices may be applied where adequate data are available. An evaluation method based on the concept of opportunity cost (i.e. the cost deriving from the missed exploitation of an opportunity) is spreading.

Although the assessment is delegated to the centres of responsibility, the expected significant variability in costs could suggest, in addition to the consideration of the regional clusters (also providing for a normalisation for them), the use of the standard costs method for national parameterisation. On assessing the benefits (in terms of effectiveness) and costs of each service, we can compare them according to the rationale shown in Table 3.1, where:

- Ct: cost of the Telemedicine service
- Cs: cost of the alternative service (hypothetically, the standard treatment in place)
- Et: index of effectiveness of the Telemedicine service
- Eg: alternative service efficacy index (in hypothesis, the standard treatment in place)

The incremental cost effectiveness ratio (ICER) is calculated according to the following formula:

$$\text{RICE} = \frac{\text{Ct} - \text{Cs}}{\text{Et} - \text{Es}}$$

However, universal rules of interpretation are unavailable, and, therefore, the choice of threshold values is not necessarily risk-free. A more aseptic interpretative approach could be to evaluate the effects on the budget, maintaining a margin of motivated discretion for the evaluators.

Table 3.1 Comparison of costs, effectiveness and possible choices

Cost comparison	Comparison of effectiveness	Choice
Ct ≤ ≥ Cs	Et < Es	Standard treatment is maintained
Ct ≤ Cs	Et ≥ Es	The Telemedicine service is implemented
Ct > Cs	Et > Es	The cost-effective incremental ratio (RICE) is calculated

Source: Italian Ministry of Health (2019) Telemedicina: linee di indirizzo nazionali. http://www.salute.gov.it. Accessed 15 January 2020

Table 3.1 shows three different scenarios where Telemedicine should or should not be implemented, according to an evaluation of costs, index of effectiveness and alternative services efficacy index

References

Ballini L, Negro A, Maltoni S et al (2015) Interventions to reduce waiting times for elective procedures. Cochrane Database Syst Rev 2(CD005610): 1–29

Censis (2017) VII Rapporto RBM Censis sulla sanità pubblica, privata e intermediata. Il futuro del Sistema Sanitario in Italia tra universalismo, nuovi bisogni di cura e sostenibilità. Censis, Rome

Centro Nazionale per la Telemedicina e le Nuove Tecnologie Assistenziali (2018) Ricognizione delle principali normative nazionali italiane dedicate alla realizzazione di servizi sanitari in Telemedicina. https://www.iss.it. Accessed 15 Jan 2020

Chen CE, Chen CT, Hu J et al (2017) Walk-in clinics versus physician offices and emergency rooms for urgent care and chronic disease management. Cochrane Database Syst Rev 2(CD011774):1–10

Communication from the Commission to the European Parliament, the Council, the European Economic and Social Committee and the Committee of the Regions on: Telemedicine for the benefit of patients, healthcare systems and society (2008), retrived from https://ec.europa.eu/transparency/regdoc/rep/1/2008/EN/1-2008-689-EN-F1-1.Pdf, on 17.05.2020

D'Andreamatteo A, Ianni L, Lega F et al (2015) Lean in healthcare: a comprehensive review. Health Policy 119(9):1197–1209

De Belvis AG, Marino M, Avolio M et al (2013) Wait watchers: the application of a waiting list active management program in ambulatory care. Int J Qual Health Care 25(2):205–212

Federfarma (2019) Pharmacy/inhabitants ratio in Italy (March 2019). https://www.federfarma.it. Accessed 15 Jan 2020

Fournier J, Heale R, Rietze L (2012) Advanced access decreases wait times in primary healthcare. Healthc Quart 15(1):64–68

Gupta D, Denton B (2008) Appointment scheduling in health care: challenges and opportunities. IIE Trans 40(9):800–819

Gutacker N, Siciliani L, Cookson R (2016) Waiting time prioritisation: evidence from England. Soc Sci Med 159:140–151

Italian Ministry of Health (2019) Telemedicina: linee di indirizzo nazionali. http://www.salute.gov.it. Accessed 15 Jan 2020

Kaplan G, Hamilton Lopez M, McGinnis JM (eds) (2015) Transforming health care scheduling and access: getting to now. The National Academies Press, Washington, DC

LaGanga LR (2011) Lean service operations: reflections and new directions for capacity expansion in outpatient clinics. J Oper Manag 29(5):422–433

Landi S, Ivaldi E, Testi A (2018) Socioeconomic status and waiting times for health services: an international literature review and evidence from the Italian National Health System. Health Policy 122(4):334–351

Litvak E, Fineberg HV (2013) Smoothing the way to high quality, safety, and economy. N Engl J Med 369(17):1581–1583

Mariotti G, Meggio A, De Pretis G et al (2008) Improving the appropriateness of referrals and waiting times for endoscopic procedures. J Health Serv Res Policy 13(3):146–151

Mariotti G, Siciliani L, Rebba V et al (2014) Waiting time prioritisation for specialist services in Italy: the homogeneous waiting time groups approach. Health Policy 117(1):54–63

Mehrotra A, Keehl-Markowitz L, Ayanian JZ (2008) Implementation of open access scheduling in primary care: a cautionary tale. Ann Intern Med 148(12):915–922

Ministero della Salute, Mappatura Nazionale. http://www.salute.gov.it. Accessed 15 Jan 2020

Mohammadshahi M, Yazdani S, Olyaeemanesh A et al (2019) A scoping review of components of physician-induced demand for designing a conceptual framework. J Prev Med Public Health 52(2):72–81

Moraros J, Lemstra M, Nwankwo C (2016) Lean interventions in healthcare: do they actually work? A systematic literature review. Int J Qual Health Care 28(2):150–165

Murray M, Berwick DM (2003) Advanced access: reducing waiting and delays in primary care. JAMA 289(8):1035–1040
Murray M, Tantau C (2000) Same-day appointments: exploding the access paradigm. Fam Prac Manag 7(8):45
Newman ED, Harrington TM, Olenginski TP et al (2004) 'The rheumatologist can see you now': successful implementation of an advanced access model in a rheumatology practice. Arthritis Care Res 51(2):253–257
Nuti S, Vainieri M (2012) Managing waiting times in diagnostic medical imaging. BMJ Open 2(6):e001255
Propper C, Sutton M, Whitnall C et al (2008) Did 'targets and terror' reduce waiting times in England for hospital care? BE J Econ Anal Policy 8(2):1–32
Propper C, Sutton M, Whitnall C et al (2010) Incentives and targets in hospital care: evidence from a natural experiment. J Public Econ 94(3–4):318–335
Rebba V (2009) I ticket sanitari: strumenti di controllo della domanda o artefici di disuguaglianze nell'accesso alle cure? Politiche Sanit 10(4):221–242
Rebba V, Rizzi D (2011) Waiting times and cost sharing for a public health care service with a private alternative: a multi-agent approach. University Ca'Foscari of Venice, Dept. of Economics Research Paper Series No. 18
Regione Lombardia (2017) 'Missione valutativa promossa dal Comitato Paritetico di Controllo e Valutazione e dalla III Commissione consiliare', Missione Valutativa n. 13/2017
Rose KD, Ross JS, Horwitz LI (2011) Advanced access scheduling outcomes: a systematic review. Arch Intern Med 171(13):1150–1159
Sampson F, Pickin M, O'Cathain A et al (2008) Impact of same-day appointments on patient satisfaction with general practice appointment systems. Br J Gen Pract 58(554):641–643
Siciliani L (2005) Does more choice reduce waiting times? Health Econ 14(1):17–23
Siciliani L (2008) A note on the dynamic interaction between waiting times and waiting lists. Health Econ 17(5):639–647
Siciliani L (2012) Domanda e offerta di servizi sanitari, priorità e tempi di attesa. Politiche Sanit 13(1):4–9
Siciliani L, Borowitz M, Moran V (eds) (2013) Waiting time policies in the health sector what works? OECD, Paris
Siciliani L, Moran V, Borowitz M (2014) Measuring and comparing health care waiting times in OECD countries. Health Policy 118(3):292–303
Van der Voort MMR, van Merode FG, Berden BH (2010) Making sense of delays in outpatient specialty care: a system perspective. Health Policy 97(1):44–52
Van der Voort MR, van Wijngaarden J, Janssen S et al (2014) Sustainability of improvements in access to outpatient specialist care in The Netherlands. J Health Serv Res Policy 19(2):94–101
Viberg N, Forsberg BC, Borowitz M et al (2013) International comparisons of waiting times in health care–limitations and prospects. Health Policy 112(1–2):53–61

Chapter 4
Reasons for the Non-Adoption of Telemedicine in Italy: An Empirical Study

Abstract The fourth and final chapter of this volume addresses the research that has emerged from the growing interest in Telemedicine in Europe and Italy. Despite the abundance of legislation that has increased accessibility to Telemedicine, especially in pharmacies, there continues to be resistance from the Italian territories, making Telemedicine in Italy an isolated and sporadic phenomenon. From the discussions in previous chapters, it can be seen that the diffusion of technological innovations in health systems is a crucial factor in the adoption of such innovations, which must be done consciously by community-based organisations. Hence, it is of interest to investigate the reasons for Italian pharmacists and owners or managers of community-based pharmacies choosing not to adopt Telemedicine. As will be seen in the course of this chapter, respondents were neither uniform nor compact. Indeed, the survey based on the Unified Theory of Acceptance and Use of Technology shows that there are profound differences among groups of respondents and a range of variables that come into play in the choice of whether or not to adopt Telemedicine. For example, the assumption that younger people would be more inclined to adopt technological innovations was not supported by the data, which showed the exact opposite. Thus, this chapter will assist both public and private decision-makers to make appropriate decisions so that Telemedicine is no longer, in Italian communities at least, an episodic and sporadic phenomenon.

Keywords Cluster analysis · SEM · Goodness-of-fit measures · Significant relations

4.1 Background and Conceptual Framework

The following specific operational objective was included in a 2019 Italian ministerial directive to define the governance of the distribution and systematic use of Telemedicine in the context of public care and assistance. The mapping methodology was prepared by a subgroup of the board of the new Health Information System,

N. Cobelli, *Innovation in Community-Based Private Practices Through eHealth*, International Series in Advanced Management Studies,
https://doi.org/10.1007/978-3-030-48177-3_4

which comprised representatives from Lombardy, Veneto, Emilia Romagna, Piedmont and Tuscany as well as the National Centre for Telemedicine and New Assistive Technologies of the Istituto Superiore di Sanità. This led to the compilation of an online questionnaire to evaluate the efficacy and cost-effectiveness of Telemedicine based on a model already used in various European projects (see Ministero della Salute 2019). The results of this ongoing study are not yet available. However, according to the Italian Higher Institute of Health, as of 2017, there were only 384 Telemedicine services distributed throughout the nation (Centro Nazionale per la Telemedicina e le Nuove Tecnologie Assistenziali 2018) compared with a much higher number of private pharmacies, which was 17,656 in 2019 (Federfarma 2019).

Although comparing numbers from 2017 to 2019 may introduce some error, it is evident that the number of pharmacies using Telemedicine services is well below the country's potential. For this reason, it is particularly interesting to investigate the reasons for the poor implementation of Telemedicine in Italy. Indeed, the mapping that was finalised in 2019 will provide a more precise picture of the number of pharmacies that have chosen to adopt Telemedicine. Rather, what we intend to investigate in this chapter are the reasons behind the choice of non-adoption of Telemedicine by community-based private pharmacies.

In light of the above considerations and the poor implementation of Telemedicine in Italy, it was decided to conduct a study aimed at investigating the reasons for the non-adoption of this new technology. With this aim, we developed a questionnaire based on the UTAUT model presented in Chap. 2 of this work (see Appendix). The definitions of the various constructs that make up the model align with those provided by the creators of the UTAUT model and are presented in succession. The paper used to define the various constructs was by Venkatesh et al. (2003) (hereafter termed 'the authors').

Performance expectancy was defined by Venkatesh et al. (2003) as the degree to which an individual believes that using a system will help him or her to improve job performance. Constructs from various models that relate to performance expectancy include perceived usefulness (TAM/TAM 2), extrinsic motivation, job fit, relative advantage (IDT) and outcome expectations. Although these constructs have evolved in the literature, some authors have acknowledged the similarities between the following: usefulness and extrinsic motivation (Davis et al. 1992), usefulness and job fit (Thompson et al. 1991), usefulness and relative advantage (Davis et al. 1992; Moore and Benbasat 1991; Plouffe et al. 2001), usefulness and outcome expectations (Compeau and Higgins 1995a; Davis et al. 1992) and job fit and outcome expectations (Compeau and Higgins 1995b). The performance expectancy construct in each individual model is the strongest predictor of intention and remains significant at all points of measurement in both voluntary and mandatory settings (Agarwal and Prasad 1998; Compeau and Higgins 1995a; Davis et al. 1992; Taylor and Todd 1995; Thompson and Yarnold 1995; Venkatesh and Davis 2000). However, from a theoretical perspective, there is reason to expect that the relationship between performance expectancy and intention will be moderated by gender and age. Research on gender differences indicates that men tend to be highly task-oriented (Minton and Schneider 1980); thus, performance expectancy with respect to task accomplishment is likely to be especially salient for men. Gender schema theory suggests that such differences stem from gender roles and socialisation processes reinforced from birth rather than biological gender per se (Bem 1981; Bem and Allen 1974; Lubinski et al. 1983; Lynott and McCandless 2000; Motowidlo 1982).

Effort expectancy is defined as the degree of ease associated with the use of a system. Three constructs from existing models capture the concept of effort expectancy: perceived ease of use, complexity and ease of use. Prior research (Davis et al. 1992; Moore and Benbasat 1991; Plouffe et al. 2001; Thompson et al. 1991) has noted substantial similarity among construct definitions and measurement scales. The effort expectancy construct in each model is significant in the contexts of both voluntary and mandatory usage; however, each is significant only during the first period, becoming non-significant over periods of extended and sustained usage, which is consistent with previous research (Agarwal and Prasad 1998; Davis et al. 1992; Thompson et al. 1991). Effort-oriented constructs are expected to be more salient in the early stages of a new behaviour, when processing issues must be overcome, and later become overshadowed by instrumentality concerns (Davis et al. 1992; Szajna 1996; Venkatesh 1999). Drawing upon other research (Bem and Allen 1974), Venkatesh and Morris (2000) suggest that effort expectancy is more salient for women than for men. As noted previously, predicted gender differences may be driven by cognition related to gender roles (Lynott and McCandless 2000; Motowidlo 1982). Increased age has been found to be associated with difficulty in processing complex stimuli and allocating attention to information on the job, both of which may be necessary when using software systems. Prior research supports the notion that constructs related to effort expectancy will be stronger determinants of individuals' intentions for women (Venkatesh and Morris 2000; Venkatesh et al. 2000) and older workers (Morris and Venkatesh 2000).

Social influence is defined as the degree to which an individual perceives that important others believe that he or she should use a new system. Social influence as a direct determinant of behavioural intention is represented as a subjective norm in TRA, TAM 2, TPB, social factors and image. Thompson et al. (1991) used the term 'social norms' to define this construct, acknowledging its similarity to subjective norms in TRA. Although they have different labels, each construct contains the explicit or implicit notion that behaviour is influenced by individuals' perceptions of how others view them as a result of using technologies.

Facilitating conditions is the degree to which an individual believes that organisational and technical infrastructure exists to support the use of a system. This definition captures concepts embodied by three different constructs: perceived behavioural control, facilitating conditions and compatibility. Each of these constructs is operationalised to include aspects of the technological and/or organisational environment designed to remove barriers to use. Taylor and Todd (1995) acknowledged the theoretical overlap by modelling facilitating conditions as a core component of perceived behavioural control in TPB. The compatibility construct incorporates items that fit between an individual's work style and the use of a system in an organisation.

Self-efficacy and *anxiety* have been modelled as direct determinants of intention, mediated by perceived ease of use (Venkatesh 2000). Consistent with this, the authors found that self-efficacy and anxiety appear to be, in some cases, significant determinants of intention.

Consistent with the underlying theory of all intention models discussed in Chap. 2, the authors expect that *behavioural intention* will have a significant positive influence on technology usage.

An additional construct, *clinical background*, has been added on the basis of previous qualitative research (Cobelli and Chiarini 2020). A crucial element identified in this study was pharmacists' fear that new technologies might invalidate their role. Thus, an understanding of whether a strong clinical background was a limiting factor in the adoption of Telemedicine is relevant because Telemedicine may potentially be perceived as a threat to the pharmacy profession.

4.2 Participants and Recruitment

The literature provides many guidelines with respect to sample size, including having (a) a minimum sample size of 100 or 200 (Boomsma 1982, 1985), (b) 5 or 10 observations per estimated parameter (Bentler and Chou 1987) or (c) 10 cases per variable (Nunnally and Bernstein 1967). Our final dataset meets all of the above criteria. Our survey was distributed to a sample of 3000 Italian pharmacists who met the following inclusion criteria:

- Possessed the title of pharmacist
- Practised the profession as the manager or owner of a pharmacy
- Practised in a private pharmacy (municipal pharmacies were excluded because of the difficulty in identifying decision-makers)
- Had not adopted Telemedicine technology
- Worked in a pharmacy with a maximum of two points of sale (to ensure that respondents were practising in a community-based pharmacy)

The questionnaire was administered by certified electronic mail through a database supplied by the Italian pharmacy association Federfarma, which regulates pharmacies operating in Italian territories. Reminder calls were made to recipients who had not yet completed the questionnaire. Overall, 671 completed questionnaires were obtained. The literature presented at the beginning of this paragraph shows that random convenience sampling of this number of potential respondents is fully justified and significant. The number of respondents was high and the response rate statistically satisfactory.

Tables 4.1, 4.2, 4.3, 4.4 and 4.5 provide detailed descriptions of the sample studied. The number of respondents totalled 671 (SD = 11,891). The vast majority of respondents were men (Table 4.2) with more than 15 years' experience (61.3%)

Table 4.1 Descriptive statistics of the sample

N	Minimum	Maximum	Mean	SD
671	25	74	50.41	11.891

Table 4.2 Gender

Gender	*n*	Percentage	Cumulative (%)
Female	187	27.9	27.9
Male	484	72.1	72.1
Total	671	100.0	100.0

Table 4.3 Experience in the profession

Years	*n*	Percentage	Cumulative (%)
<3	9	1.3	1.3
3–5	58	8.6	8.6
6–10	73	10.9	10.9
11–15	120	17.9	17.9
>15	411	61.3	61.3
Total	671	100.0	100.0

Table 4.4 Years of operation of the pharmacy

Variables (years)	*n*	Percentage	Cumulative (%)
<3	4	0.6	0.6
3–5	11	1.6	1.6
6–10	87	13.0	13.0
11–15	71	10.6	10.6
>15	498	74.2	74.2
Total	671	100.0	100.0

Table 4.5 Role of respondents

Role	*n*	Percentage	Cumulative (%)
Manager	125	18.6	18.6
Owner	546	81.4	81.4
Total	671	100.0	100.0

(Table 4.2) working in a pharmacy operating for more than 15 years (74.2%) (Table 4.3) with the role of pharmacy owner (81.4%) (Table 4.4).

Table 4.5 highlights that the vast majority of respondents (546, 81.4%) were pharmacy owners, with only 18.6% being managers. There are two reasons for this gap and the absence of employees. First, administration of the questionnaire took place via certified email, which is usually read by owners or managers. Second, it is assumed that the decision to adopt Telemedicine is made by people high in the pharmacy hierarchy.

4.3 Method

The collected data were analysed with the aim of identifying groups of Telemedicine non-users. Thus, it was decided to undertake cluster analysis (CA) using R software for statistical computing and graphics (R Core Team 2020). CA involves the grouping of a set of objects in such a way that objects in the same group (known as a cluster) are more similar to each other than to those in other clusters. CA is primarily used in exploratory data mining and is a common technique for statistical data analysis in many fields, including machine learning, pattern recognition, image analysis, information retrieval, bioinformatics, data compression and computer graphics (Anderberg 2014).

CA represents a general task to be solved rather than a specific algorithm. It may be conducted using various algorithms that differ significantly in their definition and efficient identification of clusters. Popular notions of clusters include those with short distances between cluster members, dense areas of data space, intervals and particular statistical distributions. Thus, clustering can be formulated as a multi-objective optimisation problem. The appropriate clustering algorithm and parameter settings (including distance function, density threshold or number of expected clusters) depend on the individual dataset and intended use of results. Thus, CA is not an automatic task but an iterative process of knowledge discovery or interactive multi-objective optimisation involving trial and error. It is often necessary to modify data prior to processing and model parameters until the result achieves the desired properties.

CA originated in anthropology with Driver and Kroeber (1932), was introduced to psychology by Zubin (1938) and was famously used by Cattell (1943) for trait theory classification in personality psychology. Therefore, it is a psychometric method widely used in many disciplines, including business management. Its main objective is to identify homogeneous groups of respondents and to identify the factors through which this homogeneity takes place.

In the present work, CA was conducted on a sample of pharmacists, specifically non-users of Telemedicine. Thus, the following hypotheses were developed:

H1: Non-users of Telemedicine may be divided into relatively homogeneous groups.
H2: Non-users comprise at least two distinct groups: convinced non-users and non-users more likely to adopt Telemedicine.

To confirm or reject H1 and H2, statistical k-means clustering was conducted. k-means (MacQueen 1967) is a simple unsupervised learning algorithm that groups a dataset into a user-specified number (k) of clusters. The algorithm clusters the data into k clusters, but the appropriate number of clusters is not known a priori. Therefore, it is necessary to determine the number of clusters. The following three well-known methods to validate the number of clusters were used:

- Elbow method
- Average silhouette method
- Gap statistic method

The elbow method estimates the percentage of variance explained as a function of the number of clusters. This method is based on the notion that one should choose the number of clusters so that adding another cluster does not improve the modelling of the data. The percentage of variance explained by the clusters is plotted against the number of clusters. The first clusters will provide much information, but at some point, the marginal gains will drop dramatically, creating an angle in the graph. The correct k (i.e. number of clusters) is chosen at this point, hence the 'elbow' criterion. The idea is to begin with $k = 2$, increasing k by 1 at each step to calculate the clusters and the cost that comes with training. At a certain k value, the cost will drop dramatically, reaching a plateau at which point it is increased further. This will be the desired k value. After this, the number of clusters is increased, but the new clusters will be close to some of the existing clusters (Bholowalia and Kumar 2014).

The average silhouette method is another useful means of assessing the natural number of clusters. The silhouette of a data point is a measure of how closely it is matched to other data points within its cluster and how loosely it is matched to data points of the neighbouring cluster, i.e. the cluster with the lowest average distance from the datum (Rousseeuw 1987). A silhouette close to 1 implies the datum is in an appropriate cluster, while a silhouette close to -1 implies the datum is in the wrong cluster. Optimisation techniques such as genetic algorithms are useful in determining the number of clusters giving rise to the largest silhouette (Letí et al. 2004). It is also possible to rescale the data in such a way that the silhouette is more likely to be maximised at the correct number of clusters (de Amorim and Hennig 2015).

The gap statistic method estimates the threshold and the corresponding likelihood that values above the threshold belong to the background population. Such methods can provide a complete statistical description of the threshold and its associated effectiveness. When the likelihood associated with the derived threshold is low (e.g. 0.01), the threshold is statistically significant in the sense that the corresponding probability denotes that the threshold could only occur by chance once in 100 times if there were no anomalies. Note that if the estimated probability is 0.5 or so, then the threshold is as likely as not to be found in the dataset where no anomalies are present, in which case the inference would be meaningless (Miesch 1981). The gap statistic is defined as the maximum gap between adjacent values in an ordered array after each gap has been adjusted for the expected normal frequency. The midpoint of an adjusted gap that exceeds the corresponding critical value may be taken as an estimate of the threshold (Miesch 1981), and the adjusted gap between successive values is then compared with referential critical values to determine the significance of the derived threshold (Stanley and Sinclair 1989). The gap statistic method involves the same assumption of normal distribution as the method of probability plot. It has been shown that this method is especially appropriate for separating data from two or more mixed populations, between which there are only subtle differences rather than distinct modes (Miesch 1981; Tibshirani et al. 2001; Yan and Ye 2007).

4.4 Data Analysis

As shown in Fig. 4.1, the elbow method resulted in the identification of three distinct clusters. Figure 4.2 depicts the result of the average silhouette method, which resulted in the identification of two distinct clusters. The gap statistic method, shown in Fig. 4.3, generated four possible clusters. Thus, each applied method generated a different result.

Figure 4.4 highlights the differences between the different k-means analyses with k equal to 2, 3 and 4, respectively. As can be seen, $k = 2$ is on the left, $k = 3$ is in the middle, and $k = 4$ is on the right.

Figure 4.4 shows that the three k-means analyses resulted in three different scenarios, with $k = 2$ and $k = 3$ resulting in well-defined clusters but $k = 4$ resulting in a fourth cluster with limited numbers. More precisely:

- The two-cluster version had 302 and 369 respondents, respectively, in each cluster.
- The three-cluster version had 151, 220 and 300 respondents, respectively.
- The four-cluster version had 17, 220, 143 and 291 respondents, respectively.

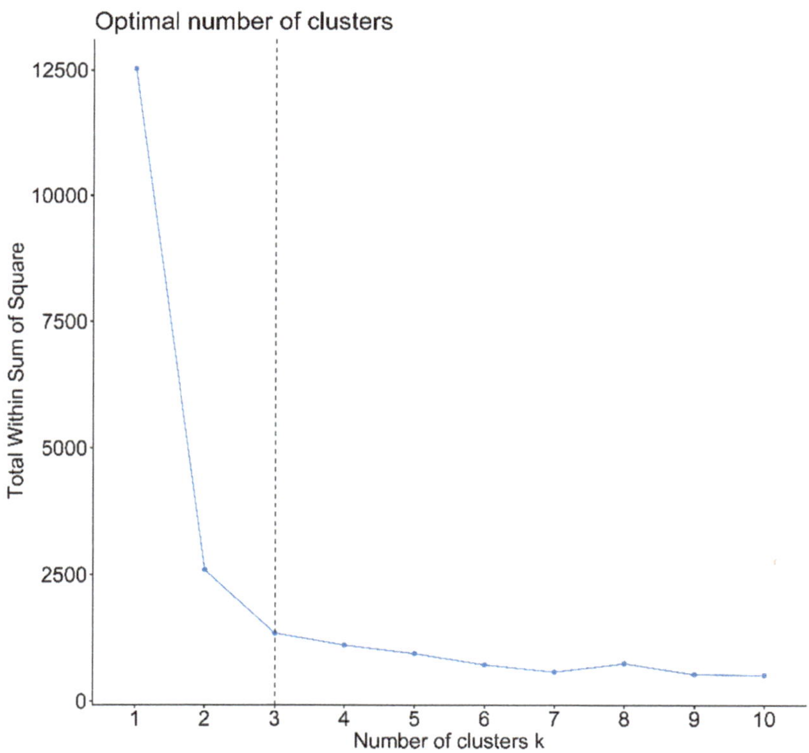

Fig. 4.1 Result of cluster analysis using the elbow method (three clusters)

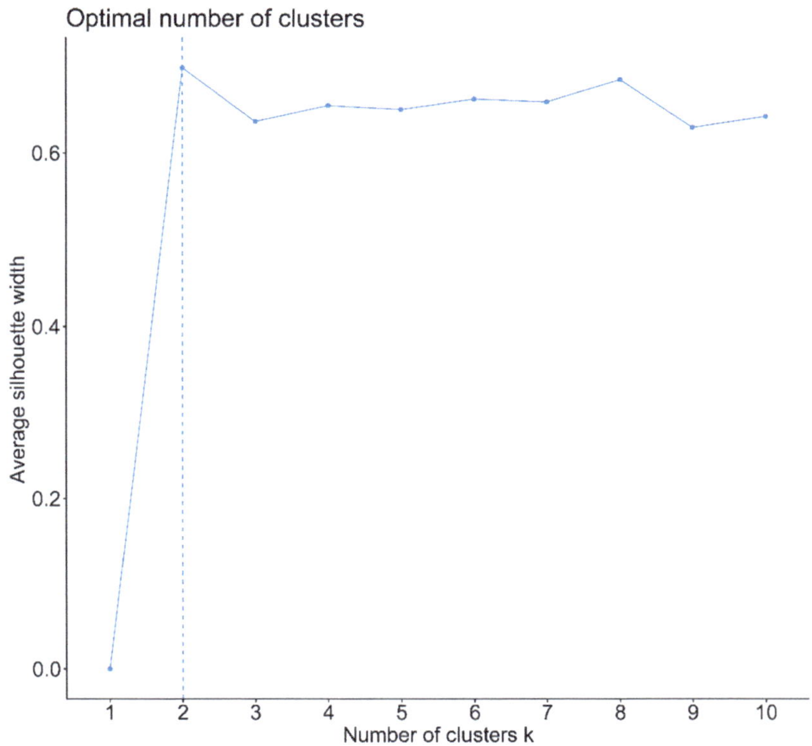

Fig. 4.2 Result of cluster analysis using the average silhouette method (two clusters)

For this reason, the $k = 4$ solution was discarded. To decide between $k = 2$ and $k = 3$, the explained variance for each cluster was evaluated:

- For k-means with two clusters, the explained variance was 79.3%.
- For k-means with three clusters, the explained variance was 89.3%.

In light of these values for explained variance, we opted for the three-cluster solution.

Figure 4.5 shows the difference between the three clusters identified through the elbow method. From the plot of the CA for $k = 3$, both H1 and H2 were confirmed. It was then possible to define three distinct groups in our sample:

- The left-hand cluster comprised pharmacists willing to adopt Telemedicine, even though adoption had not yet taken place (hereafter referred to as the 'endorsement group').
- The middle cluster comprised pharmacists who were not yet users but were close to adopting Telemedicine (hereafter referred to as the 'forthcoming adopters group').
- The right-hand cluster comprised pharmacists less likely to adopt Telemedicine (hereafter referred to as the 'reticent group').

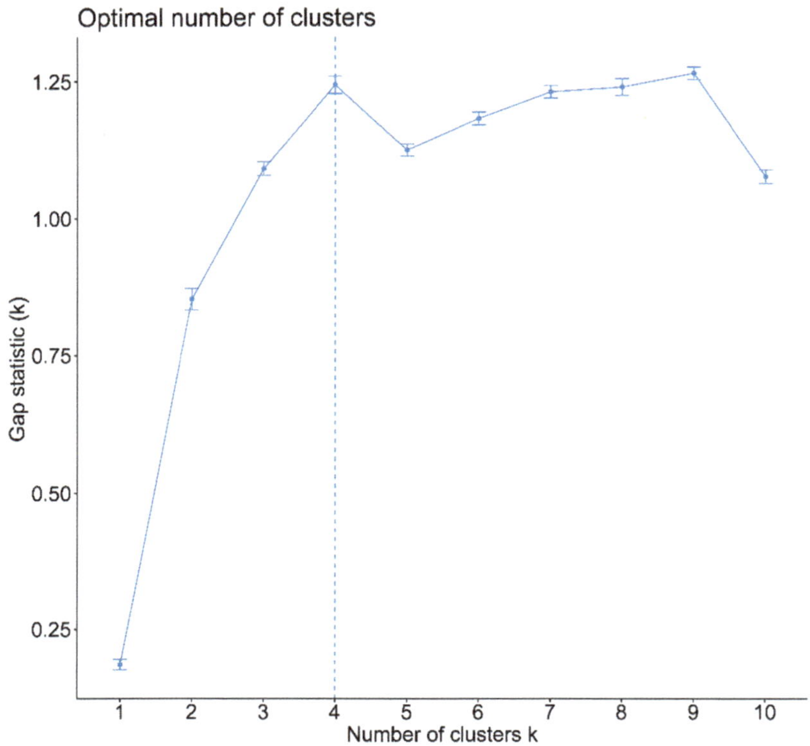

Fig. 4.3 Result of cluster analysis using the gap statistic method (four clusters)

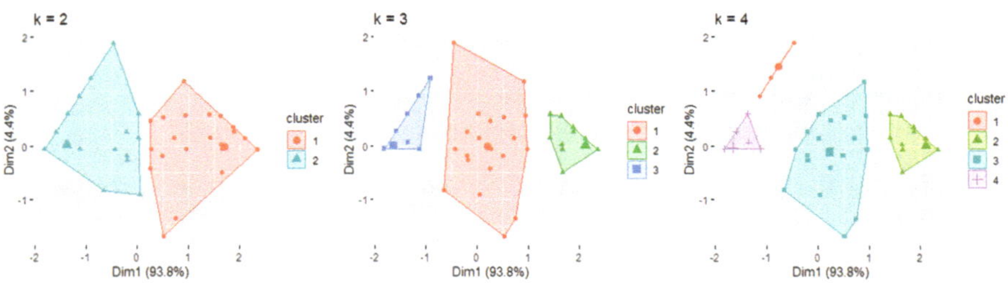

Fig. 4.4 Comparison of the three clustering methods

4.5 Findings

Once the three different groups of the investigated sample had been defined, multi-group structural equation modelling (SEM) was chosen as the statistical method to describe the internal relations within each cluster.

Various statistical and psychometric methods have been developed to study measurement invariance (Bentler et al. 1987; Byrne 1989; Cole and Maxwell 1985;

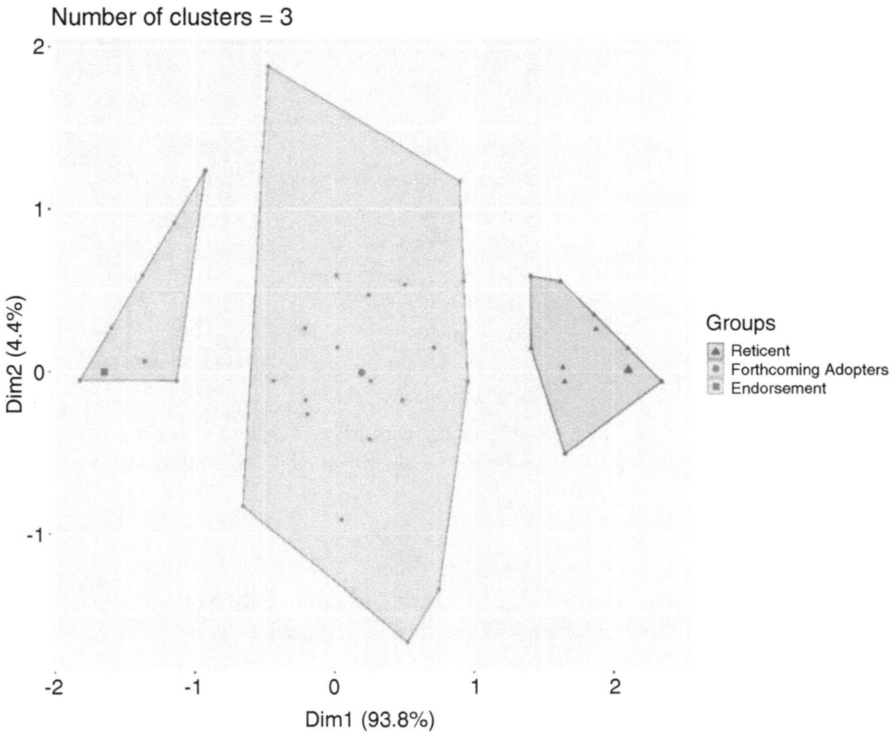

Fig. 4.5 Classification of clusters by the propensity to adopt Telemedicine

Table 4.6 Goodness-of-fit measure

Index	Good fit	Adequate fit
$\chi 2$	$0 \leq \chi 2 \leq 2\ df$	$2\ df < \chi 2 \leq 3\ df$
RMSEA	0 ≤ RMSEA ≤0.05	0.05 < RMSEA ≤0.08
CFI	0.97 < CFI ≤1.00	0.95 < CFI ≤0.92

Table 4.6 presents the main indices to evaluate good and adequate fit. $\chi 2$ refers to statistical hypothesis tests that are valid when the test statistic is chi-squared distributed under the null hypothesis (Gatignon 2010). RMSEA is root-mean-square error of approximation, which avoids sample size issues by analysing discrepancies between the hypothesised model with optimally chosen parameter estimates and the population covariance matrix (Hu and Bentler 1999). RMSEA ranges from 0 to 1, with smaller values indicating a better model fit. A value of .06 or less indicates an acceptable model fit. CFI is comparative fit index, which analyses the model fit by examining the discrepancy between the data and the hypothesised model while adjusting for issues of sample size inherent in the chi-squared test of model fit (Gatignon 2010) and the normed fit index (Tanaka 1993). CFI values range from 0 to 1, with larger values indicating a better fit. Previously, a CFI value of .90 or larger was considered to indicate an acceptable model fit (Hu and Bentler 1999). However, recent studies show that a value greater than .90 is needed to ensure that misspecified models are not deemed acceptable (Hu and Bentler 1999). Thus, a CFI value of .95 or higher is presently accepted as an indicator of good fit

Table 4.7 Model test fit

Test statistic	101,045 (adequate fit)
Degrees of freedom	36
p-value (chi-square)	0.000
Test statistic for each group	
Reticent group	45,065
Forthcoming adopters group	21,878
Endorsement group	34,102
Comparative fit index	0.970 (good fit)
Root-mean-square error of approximation (RMSEA)	0.080 (adequate fit)
90% confidence interval (lower)	0.069
90% confidence interval (upper)	0.111
p-value RMSEA ≤0.05	0.001

Table 4.7 presents the main indexes to evaluate adequate fit of the test (χ^2 and RMSEA) and good fit (CFI)

Jöreskog 1971; Lee and Tsui 1982; Millsap and Hartog 1988; Muthén 1989; Reise et al. 1993; Schmitt 1982; Sörbom 1974), all of which involve multigroup SEM (see also Yuan and Chan 2016).

Table 4.6 shows the references for the fit indices, while Table 4.7 shows the adequacy and goodness of fit of the adopted model.

Through SEM analysis, it was possible to conduct a detailed evaluation of the relationships between the constructs and between the constructs and variables in the UTAUT model for each of the three clusters identified.

4.5.1 Significant Relations in the Endorsement Group

Table 4.8 shows the significant relations between constructs and between constructs and variables (highlighted in grey). In the endorsement group, behavioural intention was influenced by facilitating conditions, anxiety and clinical background, all of which contributed to whether Telemedicine would be adopted. In other words, this cluster comprised those who would readily adopt Telemedicine if the information addressed to them was aimed at reducing their anxiety, helped them understand that Telemedicine would enrich their practice and emphasised the availability of adequate support in case of need.

In this specific cluster, *performance expectancy* was highly variable depending on gender (males were more willing to use Telemedicine than females) and role (managers showed a greater propensity to use Telemedicine compared with owners).

Table 4.8 Factors affecting endorsement group choices

Regression	Estimate	SE	*z*-value	*p*(>|*z*|)	Std. lv.	Std all.
BI						
Perf	−0.032	0.023	−1.368	0.171	0.032	0.090
Eff	−0.001	0.024	−0.023	0.981	−0.001	−0.001
Att	0.061	0.034	1.781	0.075	0.061	0.107
SI	0.025	0.024	1.020	0.308	0.025	0.068
FC***	0.153	0.026	5.833	0.000	0.153	0.348
SE	0.041	0.027	1.503	0.133	0.041	0.092
Anx***	−0.043	0.021	−2.053	0.040	−0.043	−0.113
CB***	0.064	0.033	1.924	0.054	0.064	0.102
Perf						
Gender***	−0.386	0.147	−2.617	0.009	−0.386	−0.145
Company existence***	−0.330	0.098	−3.371	0.001	−0.330	−0.189
Role***	0.327	0.164	1.995	0.046	0.327	0.107
Age***	0.299	0.100	3.000	0.003	0.299	0.179
Eff						
Gender***	−0.316	0.131	−2.416	0.016	−0.316	−0.139
Working time***	−0.166	0.072	−2.309	0.021	−0.166	−0.152
Company existence	−0.052	0.098	−0.523	0.601	−0.052	−0.034
Age***	0.177	0.088	2.003	0.045	0.177	0.124
Att						
Gender***	−0.329	0.094	−3.508	0.000	−0.329	−0.198
Working time	−0.038	0.053	−0.718	0.473	−0.038	−0.048
Company existence***	0.143	0.070	2.037	0.042	0.143	0.131
Role***	0.235	0.111	2.124	0.034	0.235	0.123
Age	0.088	0.066	1.341	0.180	0.088	0.085
SI						
Gender***	−0.333	0.143	−2.325	0.020	−0.333	−0.131
Working time	0.020	0.080	0.249	0.803	0.020	0.016
Company existence***	0.315	0.106	2.978	0.003	0.315	0.189
Role	0.121	0.167	0.723	0.470	0.121	0.041
Age	0.185	0.100	1.843	0.065	0.185	0.116
FC						
Gender	−0.208	0.123	−1.691	0.091	−0.208	−0.097
Working time	−0.102	0.068	−1.499	0.134	−0.102	−0.099
Company existence	0.090	0.093	0.964	0.335	0.090	0.064
Role	0.174	0.143	1.218	0.223	0.174	0.071
Age***	0.205	0.086	2.382	0.017	0.205	0.153
SE						
Gender***	−0.596	0.113	−5.288	0.000	−0.596	−0.282
Working time***	−0.238	0.068	−3.513	0.000	−0.238	−0.234
Company existence	0.152	0.087	1.750	0.080	0.152	0.110
Role***	−0.437	0.134	−3.247	0.001	−0.437	−0.179

(continued)

Table 4.8 (continued)

Regression	Estimate	SE	*z*-value	*p*(>|z|)	Std. lv.	Std all.
Age***	0.497	0.080	6.238	0.000	0.497	0.374
Anx						
Gender	−0.114	0.142	−0.799	0.425	−0.114	−0.046
Working time	0.074	0.074	1.006	0.314	0.074	0.063
Role***	0.354	0.172	2.061	0.039	0.354	0.125
Age***	−0.221	0.101	−2.190	0.029	−0.221	−0.143
CB						
Gender	−0.063	0.087	−0.725	0.468−	−0.063	−0.042
Company existence	0.021	0.058	0.357	0.721	0.021	0.021
Age	0.016	0.056	0.291	0.771	0.016	0.017

Table 4.8 shows the statistically significant relations (highlighted in grey) between the constructs and between constructs and variables for the endorsement group of respondents. The symbol *** is used to identify the variables with a statistical significance

BI behavioural intention, *Perf* performance expectancy, *Eff* effort expectancy, *Att* attitude, *SI* social influence, *FC* facilitating conditions, *SE* self-efficacy, *Anx* anxiety, *CB* clinical background

The years of operation of the pharmacy and the years of experience of the pharmacist were other decisive elements with respect to the propensity to adopt Telemedicine in this cluster. In general, pharmacists who were older and had more experience perceived Telemedicine as an opportunity to guarantee better earnings (*performance expectancy*).

With respect to *effort expectancy*, four variables most affected the propensity to adopt Telemedicine. Female respondents were more concerned about the effort that the implementation of Telemedicine would entail, and as age and years of experience (working time) increased, the perception of effort decreased.

In relation to the *attitude* construct, a propensity towards technology was mostly found in male subjects and in pharmacies that had been operating for longer periods. With respect to role, owners had more positive attitudes towards technology than did managers.

With respect to *social influence*, female respondents were more driven to adopt Telemedicine than were males, and social influence had more effect the longer the pharmacy had been operating. In contrast, age had an influence on facilitating conditions, meaning that as the age of respondents increased, means of facilitating the adoption of Telemedicine, including support and assistance services, increased the propensity towards the new technology.

In the *self-efficacy* construct, males, respondents with the least experience and managers placed significantly less emphasis on their abilities, which tended to decrease as the age of respondents increased.

The *anxiety* construct manifested more in owners and decreased as the age of respondents increased. Finally, the *clinical background* construct in this cluster was not statistically significant for any of the variables examined.

Figure 4.6 summarises the significant regressions between the constructs and between the constructs and variables for the endorsement group. As shown, *behavioural intention* was associated with *facilitating conditions*, *anxiety* (in reverse, as

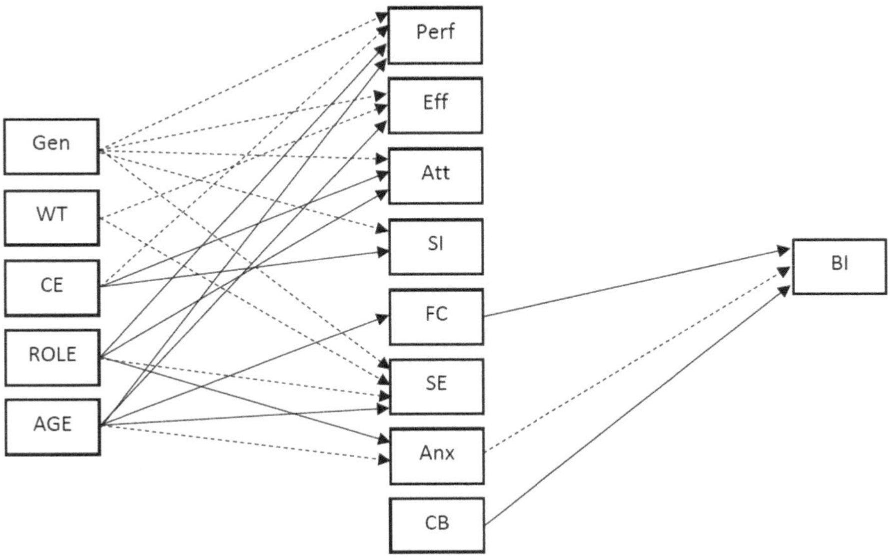

Fig. 4.6 Path diagram derived from structural equation modelling for the endorsement group Figure 4.6 shows the relations between constructs and between constructs and variables. These relations are represented by a solid arrow when the relation is direct and by a dashed arrow when the relation is inverse. *BI* behavioural intention, *Perf* performance expectancy, *Eff* effort expectancy, *Att* attitude, *SI* social influence, *FC* facilitating conditions, *SE* self-efficacy, *Anx* anxiety, *CB* clinical background

shown by the dotted arrow) and *clinical background*. In turn, these three constructs had statistically significant relations as follows:

- *Facilitating conditions* with age
- *Anxiety* with role and age
- *Clinical background* with none of the variables under examination

For the other constructs, *performance expectancy* was statistically correlated with gender, company existence, role and age; *effort expectancy* was correlated with gender, years of experience in the profession (working time) and age; *attitude* correlated to gender, years of operation of the pharmacy and role; and *social influence* correlated with gender and company existence. Finally, *self-efficacy* correlated with gender, years of work experience, role and age.

4.5.2 *Significant Relations in the Forthcoming Adopters Group*

The group of respondents categorised as forthcoming adopters shows a different set of relations between constructs and between constructs and variables compared with the cluster previously examined. The forthcoming adopters group showed a medium propensity towards Telemedicine, and the regression analysis reveals interesting cues. First, *behavioural intention* had a direct relationship with *attitude* and *self-efficacy* and an inverse relationship with *social influence* and *anxiety*. No other relations were detectable between *behavioural intention* and other examined constructs. This implies that *behavioural intention* was influenced by *attitude*, *social influence*, *self-efficacy* and *anxiety*, while the other constructs did not show any significant relation.

Table 4.9 shows the in-depth relations between constructs and between variables and constructs with statistical relevance. With respect to *performance expectancy*, statistical analysis reveals that managers had a stronger relation with the construct than did owners. With regard to *effort expectancy*, perception of effort tended to increase as experience (working time) of respondents increased. On the contrary, *effort expectancy* decreased with an increase in time of company existence. Similarly, as the age of respondents in this group increased, *effort expectancy* tended to decrease. This scenario can be explained through the years of experience of respondents: the greater the experience, the lower the effect of Telemedicine in terms of effort.

The *attitude* construct correlated only with gender—in this group, female respondents had a greater propensity to the adoption of Telemedicine compared with males. *Social influence* was correlated with role and age variables. Specifically, managers were more likely to adopt Telemedicine than were owners, and as the age of respondents increased, the propensity to use Telemedicine also increased.

Facilitating conditions was correlated with working time—the more years of experience the respondents had, the greater their propensity to adopt Telemedicine. This indicates, conversely, that those with more experience in the job expected to find services and support structures.

The *self-efficacy* construct related to the years of operation of the pharmacy in which the fewer the years of operation, the greater the propensity to adopt Telemedicine. In addition, managers were more confident, and this self-confidence increased with increasing age. In contrast, the *anxiety* construct was more closely linked to role—owners had greater anxiety around adoption than did managers.

Finally, *clinical background* was associated with the variables of gender, company existence and age. Specifically, males tended to perceive Telemedicine as an activity that did not specifically concern them as pharmacists, while women were more inclined towards Telemedicine adoption. In addition, *clinical background* was perceived as a limit to adoption when company existence decreased. Finally, in this group of respondents, it was clear that younger pharmacists were less inclined to adopt Telemedicine.

Figure 4.7 summarises the significant regressions between the constructs and between the constructs and variables for the forthcoming adopters cluster. As shown, *behavioural intention* related to *attitude*, *self-efficacy* and *anxiety*. In turn, these three constructs had statistically significant relations as follows:

- *Attitude* with gender
- *Social influence* with role and age
- *Anxiety* with role

Table 4.9 Factors affecting forthcoming adopters' choices

Regressions	Estimate	*SE*	*z*-value	*p*(>|z|)	Std. lv.	Std all.
BI						
Perf	−0.136	0.073	−1.863	0.062	−0.136	−0.206
Eff	0.024	0.069	0.348	0.728	0.024	0.029
Att***	0.226	0.058	3.909	0.000	0.226	0.330
SI***	−0.141	0.067	−2.098	0.036	−0.141	−0.200
FC	−0.046	0.077	−0.600	0.548	−0.046	−0.055
SE***	0.244	0.068	3.569	0.000	0.244	0.356
Anx***	−0.090	0.037	−2.462	0.014	−0.090	−0.197
CB	−0.074	0.084	−0.873	0.383	−0.074	−0.065
Perf						
Gender	0.166	0.200	0.832	0.405	0.166	0.067
Company existence	−0.126	0.091	−1.381	0.167	−0.126	−0.117
Role***	0.641	0.221	2.893	0.004	0.641	0.199
Age	0.060	0.126	0.475	0.635	0.060	0.042
Eff						
Gender	0.135	0.157	0.863	0.388	0.135	0.068
Working time***	−0.375	0.069	−5.423	0.000	−0.375	−0.443
Company existence***	0.196	0.075	2.615	0.009	0.196	0.228
Age***	0.227	0.098	2.323	0.020	0.227	0.199
Att						
Gender***	0.684	0.199	3.440	0.001	0.684	0.284
Working time	0.066	0.091	0.721	0.471	0.066	0.064
Company existence	0.117	0.093	1.268	0.205	0.117	0.113
Role	0.295	0.238	1.237	0.216	0.295	0.095
Age	−0.020	0.123	−0.165	0.869	−0.020	−0.015
SI						
Gender	0.225	0.178	1.264	0.206	0.225	0.097
Working time	−0.111	0.073	−1.514	0.130	−0.111	−0.112
Company existence	0.140	0.084	1.670	0.095	0.140	0.139
Role***	0.956	0.215	4.445	0.000	0.956	0.317
Age***	0.337	0.111	3.032	0.002	0.337	0.253
FC						
Gender	−0.242	0.161	−1.497	0.134	−0.242	−0.123
Working time***	0.196	0.066	2.981	0.003	0.196	0.235
Company existence	0.019	0.076	0.249	0.804	0.019	0.022
Role	0.090	0.167	0.540	0.590	0.090	0.035
Age	−0.016	0.101	−0.161	0.872	−0.016	−0.014
SE						
Gender	0.074	0.198	0.371	0.711	0.074	0.031
Working time	0.077	0.080	0.954	0.340	0.077	0.075
Company existence***	−0.195	0.095	−2.051	0.040	−0.195	−0.187
Role***	0.662	0.219	3.021	0.003	0.662	0.212

(continued)

Table 4.9 (continued)

Regressions	Estimate	*SE*	*z*-value	*p*(>|*z*|)	Std. lv.	Std all.
Age***	0.251	0.124	2.022	0.043	0.251	0.182
Anx						
Gender	−0.000	0.294	−0.001	0.999	−0.000	−0.000
Working time	−0.229	0.134	−1.710	0.087	−0.229	−0.150
Role	−1.217	0.359	−3.391	0.001	−1.217	−0.261
Age	−0.143	0.177	−0.808	0.419	−0.143	−0.070
CB						
Gender***	−0.426	0.110	−3.869	0.000	−0.426	−0.290
Company existence***	0.163	0.053	3.095	0.002	0.163	0.257
Age***	−0.304	0.070	−4.327	0.000	−0.304	−0.362

Table 4.9 shows the statistically significant relations (highlighted in grey) between the constructs and between constructs and variables for the forthcoming adopters group. The symbol *** is used to identify the variables with a statistical significance
BI behavioural intention, *Perf* performance expectancy, *Eff* effort expectancy, *Att* attitude, *SI* social influence, *FC* facilitating conditions, *SE* self-efficacy, *Anx* anxiety, *CB* clinical background

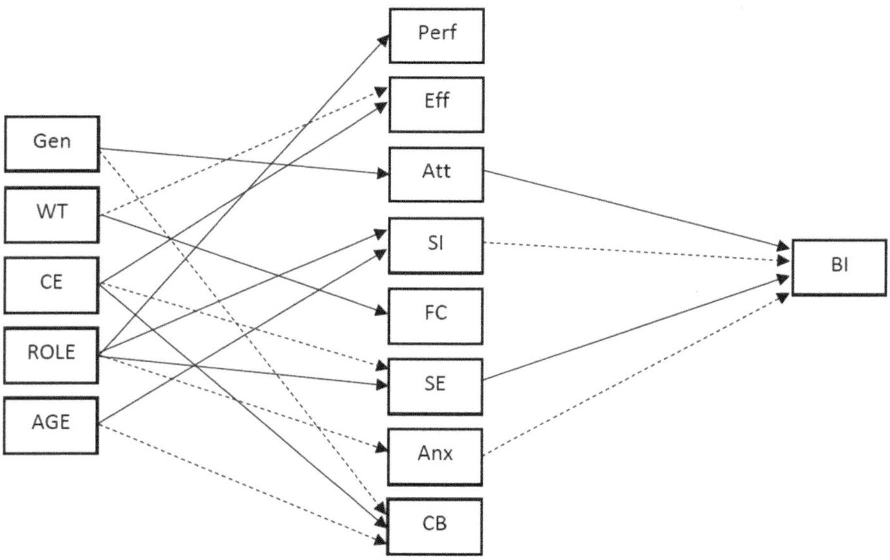

Fig. 4.7 Path diagram derived from structural equation modelling for the endorsement group Figure 4.7 shows the relations between constructs and between constructs and variables. These relations are represented by a solid arrow when the relation is direct and by a dashed arrow when the relation is inverse. *BI* behavioural intention, *Perf* performance expectancy, *Eff* effort expectancy, *Att* attitude, *SI* social influence, *FC* facilitating conditions, *SE* self-efficacy, *Anx* anxiety, *CB* clinical background

For the other constructs, *performance expectancy* was statistically correlated with role; *effort expectancy* was correlated with working time and company existence; *facilitating conditions* was correlated with working time; and *clinical background* was correlated with gender, company existence and age.

4.5.3 Significant Relations in the Reticent Group

In the group of respondents categorised as reticent, *behavioural intention* in the adoption of Telemedicine was correlated with four constructs: *performance expectancy*, *effort expectancy*, *social influence* and *clinical background*.

As shown in detail in Table 4.10, there was a general mistrust in this group about the ability of Telemedicine to generate greater profits and thus better performance. Although *social influence* increased the intention to adopt, *clinical background* was a limiting factor—it was perceived that the pharmacist's role was not compatible with the adoption of Telemedicine.

With respect to the constructs and variables, younger respondents had little confidence that Telemedicine would generate higher profits. This attitude tended to decrease as the age of respondents increased.

Effort expectancy was associated with three variables—working time, company existence and age. Specifically, as the age of respondents, years of operation of the pharmacy and years of work experience decreased, the perception of effort increased. It is likely that respondents did not perceive the adoption of Telemedicine as being worth the financial outcomes.

In contrast, *attitude* correlated with role and age—managers were more likely and younger respondents were less likely to adopt Telemedicine. Assuming that there is a perfect direct correlation ($r = 1$) between age and working time, it is unlikely that an increase in one variable would lead to a positive attitude, while an increase in the other would lead to a negative attitude. A strong correlation would indicate that the two variables—age and working time—depend on the same underlying factors. However, the data show that there was a correlation of only 0.515 and an r of 0.26 between age and working time, indicating that age variations explained only 26% of working time variation. Thus, 74% of the variation in working time was attributable to another factor. Therefore, it is likely that there were two different underlying factors, in which case one of the factors may lead to a positive attitude, while the other may lead to a negative attitude.

The *social influence* construct was correlated more with male than with female respondents, while managers were more likely to adopt Telemedicine than were owners.

With regard to *facilitating conditions*, it is clear that women and managers were more attentive to the presence of assistance and support services than were men and owners, respectively. As the age of respondents increased, the relationship between *facilitating conditions* and age tended to decrease.

Table 4.10 Factors affecting reticent group choices

Regressions	Estimate	*SE*	*z*-value	*p*(>|*z*|)	Std. lv.	Std all.
BI						
Perf***	−0.101	0.038	−2.658	0.008	−0.101	−0.245
Eff***	−0.107	0.037	−2.865	0.004	−0.107	−0.203
Att	0.005	0.025	0.196	0.844	0.005	0.017
SI***	0.172	0.036	4.769	0.000	0.172	0.428
FC	−0.052	0.028	−1.877	0.061	−0.052	−0.128
SE	0.034	0.037	0.902	0.367	0.034	0.071
Anx	0.029	0.018	1.605	0.109	0.029	0.101
CB***	−0.115	0.039	−2.920	0.003	−0.115	−0.183
Perf						
Gender	−0.000	0.186	−0.001	0.999	−0.000	−0.000
Company existence	−0.152	0.099	−1.535	0.125	−0.152	−0.103
Role	0.040	0.176	0.228	0.820	0.040	0.015
Age***	0.293	0.083	3.529	0.000	0.293	0.243
Eff						
Gender	0.080	0.133	0.598	0.550	0.080	0.039
Working time***	0.114	0.052	2.198	0.028	0.114	0.152
Company existence***	0.176	0.076	2.309	0.021	0.176	0.152
Age***	0.162	0.070	2.300	0.021	0.162	0.170
Att						
Gender	0.121	0.261	0.465	0.642	0.121	0.032
Working time***	−0.267	0.093	−2.852	0.004	−0.267	−0.194
Company existence	−0.077	0.137	−0.561	0.575	−0.077	−0.036
Role***	1.164	0.266	4.377	0.000	1.164	0.294
Age***	0.281	0.129	2.181	0.029	0.281	0.162
SI						
Gender***	−0.388	0.191	−2.031	0.042	−0.388	−0.144
Working time	−0.052	0.054	−0.968	0.333	−0.052	−0.053
Company existence	−0.079	0.103	−0.772	0.440	−0.079	−0.052
Role***	0.381	0.190	1.998	0.046	0.381	0.134
Age	0.123	0.091	1.351	0.177	0.123	0.099
FC						
Gender***	0.908	0.183	4.952	0.000	0.908	0.339
Working time	−0.054	0.072	−0.759	0.448	−0.054	−0.056
Company existence	−0.069	0.099	−0.695	0.487	−0.069	−0.046
Role***	0.768	0.184	4.166	0.000	0.768	0.273
Age***	0.177	0.092	1.921	0.055	0.177	0.144
SE						
Gender	0.190	0.159	1.196	0.232	0.190	0.084
Working time	−0.066	0.061	−1.072	0.284	−0.066	−0.079
Company existence***	0.179	0.083	2.154	0.031	0.179	0.140
Role***	0.482	0.162	2.966	0.003	0.482	0.202

(continued)

Table 4.10 (continued)

Regressions	Estimate	*SE*	*z*-value	*p*(>|z|)	Std. lv.	Std all.
Age***	0.221	0.080	2.775	0.006	0.221	0.212
Anx						
Gender***	−0.826	0.253	−3.267	0.001	−0.826	−0.220
Working time***	−0.257	0.099	−2.605	0.009	−0.257	−0.188
Role	−0.044	0.259	−0.171	0.864	−0.044	−0.011
Age***	−0.404	0.127	−3.177	0.001	−0.404	−0.235
CB						
Gender	0.156	0.117	1.328	0.184	0.156	0.090
Company existence	−0.040	0.066	−0.603	0.547	−0.040	−0.041
Age***	0.141	0.055	2.542	0.011	0.141	0.177

Table 4.9 shows the statistically significant relations (highlighted in grey) between the constructs and between constructs and variables for the reticent group. The symbol *** is used to identify the variables with a statistical significance

BI behavioural intention, *Perf* performance expectancy, *Eff* effort expectancy, *Att* attitude, *SI* social influence, *FC* facilitating conditions, *SE* self-efficacy, *Anx* anxiety, *CB* clinical background

With respect to the *self-efficacy* construct, pharmacists in companies that had been operating longer (company existence) were more confident in their abilities regarding the implementation of Telemedicine. Moreover, younger respondents felt less secure in adopting Telemedicine, and women were more confident than men in adopting Telemedicine.

The *anxiety* construct correlated with gender, where males exhibited a greater degree of anxiety and were less likely to adopt Telemedicine. In contrast, respondents with less experience showed less pronounced anxiety. Similarly, anxiety increased as the age of respondents increased.

Clinical background significantly limited the adoption of Telemedicine as the age of respondents increased.

Figure 4.8 summarises the significant regressions between the constructs and between constructs and variables for the reticent group. As shown, *behavioural intention* was correlated to *performance expectancy*, *effort expectancy*, *social influence* and *clinical background*. In turn, these four constructs were significantly correlated as follows:

- *Performance expectancy* with role
- *Effort expectancy* with working time and company existence
- *Social influence* with gender and role
- *Clinical* background with age

For the other constructs, *attitude* was statistically correlated with working time, role and age; *facilitating conditions* was correlated with gender, role and age; *self-efficacy* was correlated with company existence and role; and *anxiety* was correlated with gender, working time and age.

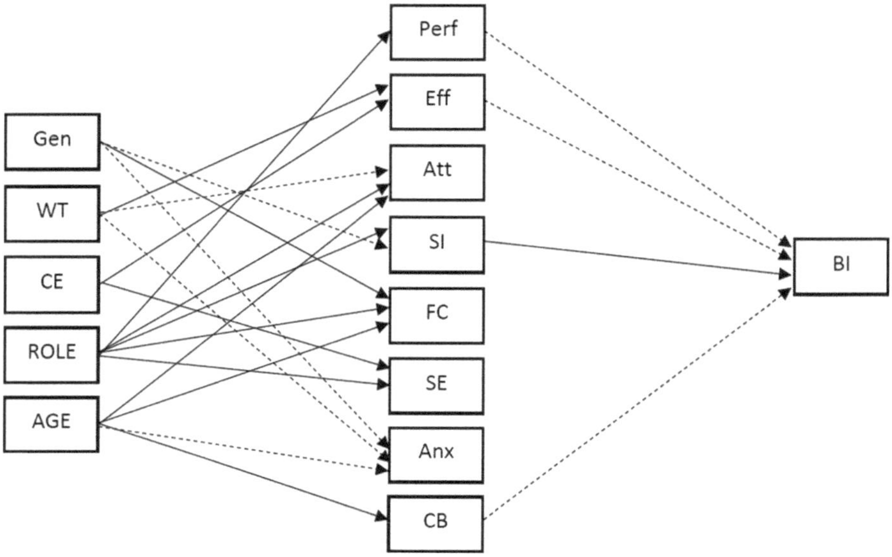

Fig. 4.8 Path diagram derived from structural equation modelling for the reticent group. Figure 4.8 shows the relations between constructs and between constructs and variables. These relations are represented by a solid arrow when the relation is direct and by a dashed arrow when the relation is inverse. *BI* behavioural intention, *Perf* performance expectancy, *Eff* effort expectancy, *Att* attitude, *SI* social influence, *FC* facilitating conditions, *SE* self-efficacy, *Anx* anxiety, *CB* clinical background

4.6 Discussion

The analysis discussed in Sects. 4.4 and 4.5 clearly shows the different propensities towards the adoption of Telemedicine in the sample of non-users. These propensities were categorised into three clusters, termed ‘endorsement group’, ‘forthcoming adopters group’ and ‘reticent group’. From the first to the third group, there was an ever-decreasing propensity for the adoption of Telemedicine, manifesting as true resistance in the reticent group. The determination of whether Telemedicine will be adopted is not black and white and cannot be done by simply distinguishing between non-adopters. Indeed, the empirical research conducted suggests a grey zone in which the level of propensity varies from possible adoption at one end to convinced non-adoption at the other.

Specifically, traits common to all three groups of non-adopters can be identified. The first trait relates to the years of experience in the pharmacy profession (working time). Specifically, the longer the experience, the lower the influence of self-efficacy, effort, facilitating conditions, attitude and anxiety. This phenomenon can be explained by a high degree of self-esteem and conviction in one’s abilities, which increases with work experience, implying that more experienced pharmacists are less concerned about their ability to adopt Telemedicine. Similarly, with respect to company existence, the more years a pharmacy had operated, the less anxiety or perceptions of effort there was with respect to the adoption of Telemedicine. In regard to facilitating conditions, this study confirms the findings of others (e.g. Cobelli and Chiarini 2020), namely, that pharmacists with greater experience had more confidence in their trade associations to offer them a rich range of support and assistance services, not only for Telemedicine.

The age variable behaved as follows: younger pharmacists had greater anxiety levels and lower self-efficacy. This is in contrast to facilitating conditions, which brought higher expectations of Telemedicine generating higher profits.

In exploring the main elements uniting the three groups of respondents, it is interesting to note those that most clearly differentiate them. The major differences were seen in relation to the gender and role of respondents.

In the endorsement group, the greatest propensity for Telemedicine was seen in male respondents and managers, who perceived Telemedicine as an opportunity for profit. In contrast, female respondents felt anxious about adoption. At the same time, however, female respondents and owners were more susceptible to social influence. This can be explained by a greater sensitivity to the community having a positive view of Telemedicine, which may be added to other services already provided by pharmacies. Overall, the intention to adopt Telemedicine in the three clusters can be clearly identified in the latent constructs *facilitating conditions* and *anxiety*.

In contrast, in the forthcoming adopters group, female respondents showed a more favourable attitude towards Telemedicine. Compared with owners, managers were more socially influenced to use Telemedicine, perceiving it as a means of generating higher profit, improving reputation and showcasing the pharmacy as meeting the customers' needs. Another element that emerged from this cluster was clinical background. Male respondents tended to consider Telemedicine as a tool unrelated to the pharmacy profession, which is consistent with the positive attitude of female respondents described above. In addition, owners had less expectations of profit, greater anxiety and lower self-esteem and were not significantly socially influenced in relation to the adoption of Telemedicine. Overall, the intention to adopt Telemedicine in the forthcoming adopters group can be clearly identified in the latent constructs *attitude*, *social influence*, *self-efficacy* and *anxiety*.

In the third and final group, the reticent group, *clinical background* was one of the main factors for non-adoption. It was significantly perceived that Telemedicine was inappropriate for or incompatible with the pharmacy profession. What also appeared to be limiting for this group was that, contrary to the other groups, an increase in respondent age was associated with increased resistance to adoption. However, there was also some diversity among the respondents in this group. In particular, female respondents and managers were relatively less reticent than were male respondents and owners. Specifically, male respondents and managers appeared more socially influenced to adopt Telemedicine, while female respondents were more anxious and more susceptible to the conditions of support and facilitation for the use of Telemedicine. Overall, the intention to adopt Telemedicine in the third cluster can be clearly identified in the latent constructs *performance expectancy*, *effort expectancy*, *social influence* and *clinical background*. For this specific group, *effort expectancy* and *clinical background* constructs strongly hindered adoption, increasing with the age of respondents.

4.7 Conclusions

In the course of this work, we set out to analyse the opportunities for eHealth, not so much from a general or legal perspective but from a purely managerial perspective. Specifically, the two determining conditions that make eHealth a future tool for healthcare systems are decentralisation of healthcare delivery and the empowerment of community-based private practice. However, these are not enough to make eHealth an attractive and intriguing phenomenon. Indeed, as seen throughout this work, in the reorganisation of health systems because of their current non-functionality in terms of costs and benefits, eHealth represents a solution from which health professionals could benefit but is often perceived as an evil rather than an opportunity.

European and Italian governments have long sought to create professional figures who can meet and satisfy the new needs of current and future patients. Likewise, institutions have passed laws that increasingly focus on decentralised and community-based healthcare systems. The reorganisation imperatives of modern health protection systems, both in terms of appropriateness of care and economic sustainability of health, have seen innovative interventions and service strategies in the traditional pharmacy sector, which in 2009, with law no. 69, was transformed into a territorial health centre better known as a 'service pharmacy'. From that moment on, both public and private pharmacies were authorised to participate in integrated home care services for residents; carry out first-instance analyses (e.g. blood sugar and blood pressure); deliver medicines and health devices to homes; schedule examinations and specialist visits in public and affiliated structures; avail patients of nurses, physiotherapists and other socio-health operators for specific services requested by family doctors or paediatricians of choice and participate in education and preventative health programmes aimed at the general population or at specific targets.

In Italy, while 2009 is considered the year of birth of pharmacies of the third millennium, 2014 was the year in which the full recognition of the roles of this pharmacy model and its contributions to territorial care and de-hospitalisation of the NHS at the institutional level took place (according to Accordo Stato Regioni of 20 February 2014, the Health Pact 2014–2016 and the Economic and Financial Document of 2015, which implements the value of the pharmacy for services for the rehabilitation of primary care).

The Accordo Stato Regioni (State Regions Conference) of 2014 produced guidelines for the launch of regional projects to deliver nationally relevant health objectives using limited resources. A review of service projects at the local level was needed to understand the weight of investment and effective use of proceeds in the new pharmacy model. This work proposes an analysis on the basis of the necessary restructuring of the pharmaceutical sector and the need to invest in resources and new professional skills by pharmacies.

In this context, eHealth encompasses a wide range of ICT applications specific to healthcare systems, which concern doctors, hospital managers, nurses, data management specialists, social security administrators and, of course, patients in the prevention or better management of disease (Buccoliero 2010).

Thus, the concept of eHealth is multidimensional and includes various disciplines and areas of development. Two of these dimensions relate to the supply and demand of current services, which include medical visits, testing, appointments and first aid. A third dimension relates to the technical infrastructure and IT equipment necessary for the provision of these services. The final dimension is cultural in that the provision and use of eHealth can only occur if an adequate digital culture is established among healthcare professionals. eHealth tools and solutions adopted in Italy include those for administrators and healthcare professionals (management information systems) as well as for citizens. In addition, they include a wide range of Telemedicine services, as seen in Chaps. 3 and 4 of this work. Ultimately, eHealth represents a real innovation to which various disciplines (IT, medicine, business economics and statistics) can contribute and for which development cannot be planned without adequate and timely knowledge of the phenomenon (European Commission 2008).

Technological innovations in the NHS are still in the early stages of development and present a heterogeneous picture, mainly because of limited coordination between the developed initiatives. This is reflected in the availability of vastly different data, both at individual healthcare institutions and at regional levels, making it difficult to follow the evolution of ICT technologies over time and compare the types and quality of digital services. This limitation in the availability of adequate data is a barrier to the development of policies to incentivise eHealth. It is necessary to study eHealth through standard indicators applicable to different territorial levels, both nationally and internationally.

In this scenario, even traditional healthcare professionals such as pharmacists, especially those in Italy who often practise in small and medium family businesses (Schmidt and Pioch 2004), can be protagonists of change. Community-based pharmacies have all the prerequisites for dispensing both drugs as well as providing an increasing number of services that were once available only in large public health facilities. Telemedicine, presented in Chaps. 3 and 4 of this volume, is one of the many tools under the wider eHealth umbrella. Although it is still new, the Italian government is broadly in favour of Telemedicine as a means of empowering pharmacies.

Of course, any change needs time for acceptance, acclimatisation and conviction. In the case of Telemedicine, it also requires a response to competition, imitation and enhancement of reputation. However, the failure to adopt Telemedicine as an eHealth tool is not necessarily linked to unfavourable views or resistance to change. Indeed, as shown by field research, there are many nuances that come into play in the psychological processes related to the propensity to adopt new technologies and which have important influences on management. In fact, latent constructs that determine a greater or lesser propensity for technological innovation are identifiable.

4.8 Managerial and Social Implications

In Italy, pharmacies continue to be heavily regulated by the regions and are characterised by a certain oligopoly in which the number of pharmacies is proportional to the number of inhabitants. Therefore, there is no true free market, making the managerial implications deduced from this work relevant.

First, it is important to understand that non-users of Telemedicine are not always convinced non-adopters. Public decision-makers and private companies supplying Telemedicine devices should understand that pharmacists will not spontaneously implement Telemedicine and other eHealth tools. This is because of the lack of real competition between pharmacies in Italy, without which owners and managers will not perceive the need to implement new types of services. Therefore, pharmacists must understand that the world changing and that trade associations play a central role in this change. As demonstrated in other studies (Cobelli and Chiarini 2020), these associations can intervene in at least two ways. First, they can promote change by inquiring and keeping their associates informed about available technological innovations that are aimed at improving the care of patients. Second, by facilitating the process of adoption of Telemedicine and other services with the aim of decentralisation and improving proximity to patients, these associations can be a point of reference for the pharmacist. Indeed, the adoption of new technologies in the Italian context cannot simply be the result of competition between players but must arise from the favourable view of the technology by pharmacy associations.

Second, public decision-makers and companies supplying devices and training for Telemedicine and other technological innovations can act from the bottom up, informing the population of the availability of new services. As demonstrated in other sectors, the pharmacy sector might be moved to change at the request of patients themselves, who, if informed of new available technologies, may become active promoters of adoption by pharmacists. However, eHealth itself has strong social connotations, and its adoption strongly affects the practice of healthcare.

The treatment of chronic disease represents a priority area for the application of Telemedicine models. Telemonitoring can improve the quality of life of chronic patients through self-management, remote monitoring solutions and early hospital discharge. Future challenges for health systems related to the ageing population, and the prevalence of chronic and post-acute disease must also be addressed through better management of the system using ICT. The introduction of Telemedicine as an innovative organisational approach would have an immediate effect on making communication between the various actors accessible and continuous, directing providers towards an appropriate use of resources; reducing the risks associated with complications, hospitalisation and waiting times and optimising the use of available resources. The availability of timely information also offers the potential for measuring and evaluating health processes through process and outcome indicators. Telemedicine tools can also be used to support drug therapy to improve compliance.

Innovation is an integral part of human history and is the engine of social development, not only for companies but also, and above all, for society, which receives it and further shapes it according to need. It is now a reality that new digital technologies have the potential to change people's lives, even in social gatherings, by offering new communication possibilities and acting directly for the benefit of a collective society. There is much hope that Telemedicine can be one of these new technologies, especially given the current economic and social landscape. eHealth, particularly Telemedicine, is a valid tool to improve public health, which now, more than ever, needs technological and cultural changes to compensate for the lack of resources. Given the increase in life expectancy and the consequent increase in chronic and post-acute disease, it is necessary to divert patients away from hospitals, and scientific technologies may be the means to overcome today's societal problems. Continuity of home care and the daily monitoring of patients with chronic disease can only improve their quality of life by reducing stress and increasing health awareness. However, Telemedicine can no longer be thought of as simply technological—it also includes social, political and economic aspects, and synergy of intent is needed between its various components. Without adequate political, legislative and economic support, the modernisation of the health system becomes impossible, and without adequate restructuring such as national broadband coverage, Telemedicine services will be useless.

By improving healthcare systems and increasing awareness of Telemedicine, it will be necessary to implement a wider range of projects involving an increasing number of patients to generate more comprehensive conclusions from various points of view. Initially, this may seem overwhelming, but it is important to consider the benefits and cost savings that will result in years to come. Telemedicine services may also lead to integration with Europe so desired by the European Parliament, with the circulation of information and knowledge being the main backbone of Telemedicine services. Italy, which comprises many rural locations, is appropriate for the development of a technology that will enable a decrease in travel distances and time, especially for the elderly and chronically ill, reduced inconvenience for family and relatives and a clear reduction in both public and private expenses.

4.9 Limitations and Future Opportunities for Research

As with any research, this work has its limitations. First, convenience sampling was used to maximise the survey response rate; thus, it may be argued that only pharmacists with an interest in the study made contact with the researchers, creating the possibility of selection bias. Second, the criteria for identifying participants were narrow, which may have affected the results emerging from the investigated sample. Finally, only pharmacists who had not yet adopted eHealth tools, specifically Telemedicine, were investigated.

Hence, there is great potential for future research opportunities. For example, it would be interesting to compare responses from pharmacists who have adopted

Telemedicine with those from non-adopters. Studies should also be conducted in other locations and countries using different sampling methodologies to ascertain the generalisability of our results. In addition, reasons for the poor market penetration and adoption of eHealth tools in Italy may be related to factors associated with differences in the roles played by Italian health actors compared with other countries. The extension of these results to different empirical settings would also provide a better understanding of how the uptake of eHealth tools might be fostered in the context of improving the quality of life of a large part of the Italian population.

Further studies are also needed to test an expanded model that considers other possible relevant factors that may be related to eHealth adoption. In particular, it would be interesting to investigate how to foster interprofessional cooperation to develop a service network among healthcare professionals based on a holistic consumer-centric perspective (Cobelli et al. 2014; Gill et al. 2011).

Another research opportunity would be to investigate the efficacy of alternative strategies to support the adoption of eHealth. For instance, a body of evidence has shown that the disclosure of illness by celebrities can increase public interest in the disease and positively influence public attitudes and behaviours (Brown and de Matviuk 2010; Hilton and Hunt 2010; Stryker et al. 2010). A similar result may be obtained for eHealth adoption and use.

In conclusion, although the technological innovation represented by eHealth is at the forefront, much remains to be studied and understood about the psychological and managerial mechanisms for the adoption and use of this technology in community-based private practice. This work represents a starting point from the managerial perspective for the healthcare professionals and patients of tomorrow.

Appendix: Questionnaire Administered to Pharmacists

We kindly ask you to freely express your degree of agreement/disagreement with respect to the following statements on a scale from 1 to 7 (where 1 = strongly disagree; 3 = neutral; 7 = disagree) in relation to Telemedicine.

Performance expectancy (Perf)
I would find Telemedicine useful in my job
Using Telemedicine would enable me to accomplish tasks more quickly
Using Telemedicine would increase my productivity
If I used Telemedicine, I would increase my chances of getting a raise
Effort expectancy (Eff)
My interaction with Telemedicine would be clear and understandable
It would be easy for me to become skilful at using Telemedicine
I would find Telemedicine easy to use
Learning to operate Telemedicine would be easy for me
Attitude towards using technology (Att)

Using Telemedicine would be a good idea
Telemedicine would make my work more interesting
Working with Telemedicine would be fun
I would like to work with Telemedicine
Social influence (SI)
People who influence my behaviour think that I should use Telemedicine
People who are important to me think that I should use Telemedicine
The Local Pharmacists Association would be helpful in the use of Telemedicine
In general, my staff would be supporting the use of Telemedicine
Facilitating conditions (FC)
I would have the resources necessary to use Telemedicine
I would have the knowledge necessary to use Telemedicine
Telemedicine is not compatible with other systems I use
A specific person (or group) would be available for assistance with Telemedicine
Self-efficacy (SE)
I could complete a job or a task using Telemedicine if I could call someone for help if I got stuck
I could complete a job or a task using Telemedicine if I had a lot of time to complete the job for which the new technology (Telemedicine) was provided
If I could call someone for help if I got stuck, I would use Telemedicine
If I had a lot of time to complete the job for which the software provided, I would use Telemedicine
If I had just the built-in help facility for assistance, I would use Telemedicine
Anxiety (Anx)
I feel apprehensive about using Telemedicine
It scares me to think that I could lose a lot of information using Telemedicine by hitting the wrong key
I hesitate to use Telemedicine for fear of making mistakes I cannot correct
Telemedicine is somewhat intimidating to me
Behavioural intention to use Telemedicine (BI)
I intend to use Telemedicine in the next months
I predict I would use Telemedicine in the next months
I plan to use Telemedicine in the next months
Clinical background (CB)
My profession is compatible with Telemedicine
Telemedicine could weaken my profession
A pharmacist should not have to think about Telemedicine
Demographics
Gender (male/female)
Age
How long have you been working in this industry? (Working time)
How long has your company been existing? (Company existence)
What is your role in the pharmacy? (owner/manager)

Source: Adapted from Venkatesh et al. (2003)
This questionnaire was administered with a brief introductory explanation of Telemedicine as well as its relevant services according to Italian law

References

Agarwal R, Prasad J (1998) A conceptual and operational definition of personal innovativeness in the domain of information technology. Inf Syst Res 9(2):204–215

de Amorim RC, Hennig C (2015) Recovering the number of clusters in data sets with noise features using feature rescaling factors. Inf Sci 324:126–145

Anderberg MR (2014) Cluster analysis for applications: probability and mathematical statistics: a series of monographs and textbooks. Academic press, Cambridge (USA)

Bem SL (1981) The BSRI and gender schema theory: a reply to Spence and Helmreich. Psychol Rev 88(4):369–371

Bem DJ, Allen A (1974) On predicting some of the people some of the time: the search for cross-situational consistencies in behavior. Psychol Rev 81(6):506–520

Bentler PM, Chou C-P (1987) Practical issues in structural modeling. Sociol Methods Res 16(1):78–117

Bentler PM, Lee SY, Weng LJ (1987) Multiple population covariance structure analysis under arbitrary distribution theory. Commun Stat Theory Methods 16(7):1951–1964

Bholowalia P, Kumar A (2014) EBK-means: a clustering technique based on elbow method and k-means in WSN. Int J Comput Appl 105(9):17–24

Boomsma A (1982) The robustness of LISREL against small sample sizes in factor analysis models. In: Jöreskog KG, Wold HOA (eds) Systems under indirect observation: causality, structure, prediction. North-Holland, Amsterdam, pp 149–173

Boomsma A (1985) Nonconvergence, improper solutions, and starting values in LISREL maximum likelihood estimation. Psychometrika 50(2):229–242

Brown WJ, de Matviuk MA (2010) Sports celebrities and public health: Diego Mardona's influence on drug use prevention. J Health Commun 15(4):358–373

Buccoliero L (2010) E-health 2.0: Tecnologie per il patient empowerment. Mondo Digitale 9(4):3–17

Byrne BM (1989) Multigroup comparisons and the assumption of equivalent construct validity across groups: methodological and substantive issues. Multivar Behav Res 24(4):503–523

Cattell RB (1943) The description of personality: basic traits resolved into clusters. J Abnorm Soc Psychol 38(4):476–506

Centro Nazionale per la Telemedicina e le Nuove Tecnologie Assistenziali (2018) Ricognizione delle principali normative nazionali Italiane dedicate alla realizzazione di servizi sanitari in Telemedicina. Available via Instituto Superiore di Sanità. http://sinc-italia.it/pdf/documento_ricognizione_normative_telemedicina_26gen2018.pdf. Accessed 20 Jan 2020

Cobelli N, Chiarini A (2020) Can value co-creation in SMEs be obtained through mHealth service digitalization? Paper presented at the 22nd Excellence in services international conference, Perrotis College, Thessaloniki, Greece, 29–30 Aug 2019

Cobelli N, Gill L, Cassia F et al (2014) Factors that influence intent to adopt a hearing aid among older people in Italy. Health Soc Care Community 22(6):612–622

Cole DA, Maxwell SE (1985) Multitrait-multimethod comparisons across populations: a confirmatory factor analytic approach. Multivar Behav Res 20(4):389–417

Compeau DR, Higgins CA (1995a) Application of social cognitive theory to training for computer skills. Inf Syst Res 6(2):118–143

Compeau DR, Higgins CA (1995b) Computer self-efficacy: development of a measure and initial test. MIS Q 19(2):189–211

Core Team R (2020) R: a language and environment for statistical computing. R Foundation for Statistical Computing, Vienna

Davis FD, Bagozzi RP, Warshaw PR (1992) Extrinsic and intrinsic motivation to use computers in the workplace. J Appl Soc Psychol 22(14):1111–1132

Driver HE, Kroeber AL (1932) Quantitative expression of cultural relationships. University of California Press, Berkeley

European Commission (2008) ICT standards in the health sector: current situation and prospects. https://ec.europa.eu/digital-single-market/en/news/ict-standards-health-sector-current-situation-and-prospects. Accessed 9 March 2020

Federfarma (2019) Pharmacy/inhabitants ratio in Italy (March 2019). https://www.federfarma.it. Accessed 15 Jan 2020

Gatignon H (2010) Statistical analysis of management data, 2nd edn. Springer, New York

Gill L, White L, Cameron ID (2011) Service co-creation in community-based aged healthcare. Manag Serv Qual 21(2):152–177

Hilton S, Hunt K (2010) Coverage of Jade Goody's cervical cancer in UK newspapers: a missed opportunity for health promotion? BMC Public Health 10(1):368

Hu LT, Bentler PM (1999) Cutoff criteria for fit indexes in covariance structure analysis: conventional criteria versus new alternatives. Struct Equ Model 6(1):1–55

Jöreskog KG (1971) Simultaneous factor analysis in several populations. Psychometrika 36(4):409–426

Lee SY, Tsui KL (1982) Covariance structure analysis in several populations. Psychometrika 47(3):297–308

Lletí R, Ortiz MC, Sarabia LA et al (2004) Selecting variables for k-means cluster analysis by using a genetic algorithm that optimises the silhouettes. Anal Chim Acta 515(1):87–100

Lubinski D, Tellegen A, Butcher JN (1983) Masculinity, femininity, and androgyny viewed and assessed as distinct concepts. J Pers Soc Psychol 44(2):428–439

Lynott PP, McCandless NJ (2000) The impact of age vs. life experience on the gender role attitudes of women in different cohorts. J Women Aging 12(1–2):5–21

MacQueen JB (1967) Some methods for classification and analysis of multivariate observations. In: Le Cam LM, Neyman J (eds) Proceedings of the fifth Berkeley symposium on mathematical statistics and probability, vol 1. University of California Press, Berkeley, pp 281–297

Miesch AT (1981) Estimation of the geochemical threshold and its statistical significance. J Geochem Explor 16(1):49–76

Millsap RE, Hartog SB (1988) Alpha, beta, and gamma change in evaluation research: a structural equation approach. J Appl Psychol 73(3):574–584

Ministero della Salute (2019), http://www.salute.gov.it, Retrieved 15 January 2020.

Minton HL, Schneider WF (1980) Differential psychology. Waveland Press, Long Grove

Moore GC, Benbasat I (1991) Development of an instrument to measure the perceptions of adopting an information technology innovation. Inf Syst Res 2(3):192–222

Morris MG, Venkatesh V (2000) Age differences in technology adoption decisions: implications for a changing work force. Pers Psychol 53(2):375–403

Motowidlo SJ (1982) Relationship between self-rated performance and pay satisfaction among sales representatives. J Appl Psychol 67(2):209–213

Muthén B (1989) Multiple-group structural modelling with non-normal continuous variables. Br J Math Stat Psychol 42(1):55–62

Nunnally JC, Bernstein IH (1967) Psychometric theory. McGraw-Hill, New York

Plouffe CR, Hulland JS, Vandenbosch M (2001) Richness versus parsimony in modeling technology adoption decisions—understanding merchant adoption of a smart card-based payment system. Inf Syst Res 12(2):208–222

Reise SP, Widaman KF, Pugh RH (1993) Confirmatory factor analysis and item response theory: two approaches for exploring measurement invariance. Psychol Bull 114(3):552–556

Rousseeuw PJ (1987) Silhouettes: a graphical aid to the interpretation and validation of cluster analysis. J Comput Appl Math 20:53–65

Schmidt RA, Pioch EA (2004) Community pharmacies under pressure: issues of deregulation and competition. Int J Retail Distrib Manag 32(7):354–357

Schmitt N (1982) The use of analysis of covariance structures to assess beta and gamma change. Multivar Behav Res 17(3):343–358

Sörbom D (1974) A general method for studying differences in factor means and factor structure between groups. Br J Math Stat Psychol 27(2):229–239

Stanley CR, Sinclair AJ (1989) Comparison of probability plots and the gap statistic in the selection of thresholds for exploration geochemistry data. J Geochem Explor 32(1–3):355–357

Stryker JE, Fishman J, Emmons KM et al (2010) Cancer risk communication in mainstream and ethnic newspapers. Prev Chronic Dis 6(1):A23

Szajna B (1996) Empirical evaluation of the revised technology acceptance model. Manag Sci 42(1):85–92

Tanaka JS (1993) Multifaceted conceptions of fit in structural equation models. In: Bollen KA, Long JS (eds) Testing structural equation models. Sage, Newbury Park, pp 10–39

Taylor S, Todd PA (1995) Understanding information technology usage: a test of competing models. Inf Syst Res 6(2):144–176

Thompson DA, Yarnold PR (1995) Relating patient satisfaction to waiting time perceptions and expectations: the disconfirmation paradigm. Acad Emerg Med 2(12):1057–1062

Thompson RL, Higgins CA, Howell JM (1991) Personal computing: toward a conceptual model of utilization. MIS Q 15(1):125–143

Tibshirani R, Walther G, Hastie T (2001) Estimating the number of clusters in a data set via the gap statistic. J R Stat Soc Series B Stat Methodol 63(2):411–423

Venkatesh V (1999) Creation of favorable user perceptions: exploring the role of intrinsic motivation. MIS Q 23(2):239–260

Venkatesh V (2000) Determinants of perceived ease of use: integrating control, intrinsic motivation, and emotion into the technology acceptance model. Inf Syst Res 11(4):342–365

Venkatesh V, Davis FD (2000) A theoretical extension of the technology acceptance model: four longitudinal field studies. Manag Sci 46(2):186–204

Venkatesh V, Morris MG (2000) Why don't men ever stop to ask for directions? Gender, social influence, and their role in technology acceptance and usage behavior. MIS Q 24(1):115–139

Venkatesh V, Morris MG, Ackerman PL (2000) A longitudinal field investigation of gender differences in individual technology adoption decision-making processes. Organ Behav Hum Decis Process 83(1):33–60

Venkatesh V, Morris MG, Davis GB et al (2003) User acceptance of information technology: toward a unified view. MIS Q 27(3):425–478

Yan M, Ye K (2007) Determining the number of clusters using the weighted gap statistic. Biometrics 63(4):1031–1037

Yuan KH, Chan W (2016) Measurement invariance via multigroup SEM: issues and solutions with chi-square-difference tests. Psychol Methods 21(3):405–426

Zubin J (1938) A technique for measuring like-mindedness. J Abnorm Soc Psychol 33(4):508–516

MIX

Papier | Fördert gute Waldnutzung

FSC® C083411

Kolibri 360 GmbH
Ferdinand-Jühlke-Straße 7
99095 Erfurt, Deutschland
produktsicherheit@kolibri360.de